W9-AZI-068

PRAISE FOR

Diversity at Work:
The Business Case for Equity

"Wilson has applied his skill as a communicator to one of the most inflammatory subjects of our time—equity. His analysis is illuminating and the case studies point to rational approaches to equity that go past the legislative debate."

> —William R. Watson
> Partner
> Baker & McKenzie (International Law Firm)

"*Diversity at Work* is a thoughtful analysis that will help any organization deal with one of the most pressing issues employers must face today. It will help organizations see more clearly how to take new action to tackle some very difficult issues surrounding managing differences in today's work environment."

> —Gerry Phillips
> Member of Provincial Parliament & Former Minister of Labour
> Province of Ontario

"Valuing diversity is a major priority at Sunnybrook....The methods outlined in this book really work!"

> —Tom R. Closson
> President & CEO
> Sunnybrook Health Science Centre

"The depth and breadth of *Diversity at Work* clearly sets the tone for a new imperative in human resources utilization and wisdom in employment practices. The linkage between diversity strategy and business planning will definitely be a leading advantage for successful business competition. This book not only offers common sense reasons for employers to take advantage of the best human resources, but it strengthens valid business decisions for employers to identify their own unique rationale for embracing *Diversity at Work*."

> —Janet Naido
> Manager, Workplace Diversity
> LCBO

TREVOR WILSON is Canada's leading consultant specializing in diversity management and employment equity. He is the President of TWI Inc. His firm's clients include some of North America's largest and most progressive employers, including: IBM, Nortel, Ernst and Young, SHL/MCI Systemhouse and Bell Canada. Wilson also won a world-wide search to work on a major diversity educational project for one of South Africa's largest employers, South African Brewery (SAB). Before founding TWI Inc. in 1996, Trevor Wilson was the President of Omnibus Consulting. Trevor has held several posts in the Ontario government, advising on issues of multiculturalism, race relations and human rights. He has been active in community affairs, serving on the City of Toronto Mayor's Committee on Race Relations, as Vice-President of Government Affairs for the African-Canadian Entrepreneurs, as well as the board of directors for the United Way of Greater Toronto. Trevor has been profiled often by the media, including the *Financial Post Magazine*, *Venture*, the *Toronto Star* and the *Globe and Mail*.

MARY ANN SAYERS, former Organizational Development Manager for Coca-Cola Beverages Ltd., has over seventeen years of marketing, advertising, and communications experience. Her clients have included such major corporations as Coca-Cola Beverages Ltd., Manulife Insurance, Mary Kay Cosmetics, and Vickers & Benson Advertising. She has a degree in Journalism and a background in Human Resource Management.

Diversity at WORK

Diversity at WORK

The Business Case for Equity

TREVOR WILSON

With Case Studies by
Mary Ann Sayers

Foreword by

DAVID M. WILLIAMS

President,
National Grocers Co. Ltd.,
Loblaws Supermarkets Limited

JOHN WILEY & SONS

Toronto • New York • Chichester • Weinheim • Brisbane • Singapore

John Wiley & Sons Canada Limited

6045 Freemont Blvd.
Missisauga, ON
L5R 4J3

Canadian Cataloguing in Publication Data

Wilson, Trevor, 1957–
  Diversity at work : the business case for equity

Includes index.
ISBN 0-471-64277-0

1. Diversity in the workplace. 2. Diversity in the workplace–
Canada. I. Sayers, Mary Ann. II. Title.
HF5549.5.M5W54 1997   658.3'04   C97-932431-9

Production Credits

Cover design: JAQ, RGD
Text design: Christine Kurys, RGD
Printer:Trigraphic

Printed in Canada
10 9 8

DEDICATION

Dedicated to my mother, Ophelia Lois Wilson who taught me about love. To my father Harry Constantine Wilson who taught me about faith — not through his words but through his deeds.

CONTENTS

FOREWORD

In the past few years, and most notably in recent months, there has been a lot of discussion (and numerous articles written) about employment equity and diversity. If you have read a sampling of the articles written, you will find that many of them emphasize the importance of equity and diversity. However, few of them express in real terms why these issues are important. Maybe the reason is in part the perception that employment equity has been a government directive and not a business imperative.

To appreciate the business case for diversity and equity one need only look at what has happened in Canada with regards to shifting immigration patterns. Traditionally, most immigrants to Canada came from Europe and the United States. Today, only 20 percent of new immigrants come from these sources. The other 80 percent come from more diverse regions (Africa and the Pacific Rim, for example). These new Canadians come with very different needs, values, and cultural beliefs which will affect when, how, and what products and services they are looking for.

The companies that are going to succeed are those that recognize these changes, and positively and proactively respond to these opportunities as they present themselves.

I believe that it makes good business sense to have a well-integrated diversity and equity program within any organization. Creating a fair and equitable work environment that recognizes and accommodates the diversity of all customers and employees can tip the balance in your favour. It will allow you to draw from a wider, more qualified talent pool of prospective employees, which translates into greater understanding and knowledge within your organization of the customers you will be serving.

This book has a message, as well as many lessons and solutions that I hope every business person in North America heeds, learns from, and uses.

I have greatly admired Trevor Wilson's contributions in bringing about a more equitable and diverse business environment through education. His methods and principle are in alignment with where the Canadian economy needs to move. As businesses, don't we want to reach, attract, and maintain as many customers as possible? Of course we do. So it stands to reason that our workplaces should reflect the customers and communities we are serving.

The truth is that we need to celebrate our diversity instead of being afraid that ever increasing numbers of people around us do not look or dress or talk the same way that we as individuals might. This should be exciting, not frightening.

At National Grocers, we came to a realization that if we wanted to continue to grow and prosper, if we wanted to attract and retain the best possible work force, then we needed to bring about change in the way we treated our most valuable commodities—our customers and employees.

We had to recognize that the issues were ours to address, and we needed to be proactive. We had to bring meaning and life to a subject that is very sensitive. We needed to realize that this issue of equity is not just about women and visible minorities, it is about everybody. We had to engage everyone openly in order to deal with the issues.

One of our more critical success factors was to ensure that our management team was informed and onside. It was important that our senior people saw issues of equity and diversity as company concerns, not only the concerns of individual employees. To initiate and create a forum for discussion, we took our management team through the diversity workshop. We all had to agree collectively that whether intentional or unintentional, there were discriminatory practices and processes in place that were part of our corporate culture. Then we had to acknowledge that there was an opportunity for us to change and become part of the solution, rather than be perceived as part of the problem.

We followed a process—the one that you will read about in this book. We worked at eliminating barriers so that a more caring, sensitive, and responsive culture could emerge. It was a common-sense approach, whereby we recognized the issues, and faced the challenge of implementing systems and procedures that accommodate the needs and values of individual employees.

It is abundantly clear that change is required in the employment systems of Canadian organizations. How to change is where we need help. There is a process of change at work in implementing diversity and equity programs, just as there is in improving manufacturing processes or the delivery of goods and services. In this book, Trevor Wilson and Mary Ann Sayers provide the roadmap for change, for growth, and for prosperity. They have my respect and thanks.

DAVID WILLIAMS
PRESIDENT AND CEO
NATIONAL GROCERS CO. LTD.

PREFACE

Not too long ago I walked into the training room of an organization to conduct a Diversity Education workshop. The room appeared to be similar to the thousand of training rooms I had entered over the past few years. There was a group of about thirty managers not so eagerly awaiting the start of a "mandatory attendance" workshop about something called Diversity. There were the usual hushed conversations and the routine jokes about sexual harassment, "getting diversified," and reverse discrimination.

As I was putting my overheads together the Human Resources Manager passed me a note which read:

"Dear Trevor, There are two people in your class that refuse to listen to a black speaker all day. We have made them a deal—they only have to stay for half, and, if they choose, may forego the afternoon. Have a great day."

"This is interesting," I thought. In fact, quite unique. This was the first overt prejudice I had faced in years after conducting this type of presentation to over ten thousand people. I wondered how it would affect the day? But, to my surprise, both people chose to remain for the entire workshop.

This story has a lot to do with the motivation behind this book. Neither of these guys were really "bad people," i.e., Archie Bunker types who hated blacks. They were just confused. Confused about the whole diversity message. They may have thought that it was about reverse discrimination or tokenism or quotas or a combination of any other sensational media story that has been written about diversity. But they were wrong, and in the final analysis not vastly dissimilar to the majority of people.

This book is about clearing the air. About getting back to what the issue of diversity is really about. In order for diversity to work it must be about business. It is not about correcting a past imbalance, being a good corporate citizen, or even about some law. It is about leveraging our country's most important strategic competitive resource—our people. And now, more than ever, it is necessary for Canada and North America to do this.

As we continue down the road of globalization and open trade, competition from non-traditional sources is increasing in every marketplace. Technology is easily transferred and duplicated across borders making it an unreliable competitive weapon. Real competitive advantage must be sustainable and not easily duplicated. The maximum utilization of human resources is the answer. That is what diversity is about. That is what this book is about.

There are some very important lessons in this book. In Chapter 1 you will see the basic distinction between equality and equity. You will learn how inequity can be caused by simply treating people the same and ignoring their differences. Diversity is about acknowledging differences instead of ignoring them. When you acknowledge a person's differences you can then treat them equitably or fairly.

In Chapter 2 the difference between real equity and what we have dubbed "legislated fairness" will be uncovered. You will see how legislated fairness across North America has failed to force people to be fair and distorted the diversity message. You will learn about the slow demise of legislated fairness across North America and at the same time the advent of diversity as the business approach.

In Chapter 3 you will be introduced to the Equity Continuum and the various approaches to diversity. You will see the model of the business case for equity. You will see that the secret behind a creative and effective diversity strategy is to go well past the law and build a program that is more progressive than any government bureaucrat could ever dream.

In Chapter 4 you will learn about the Canadian advantage. What we in Canada have learned about diversity by watching thirty years of legislated fairness in the United States. Why some of the most progressive employers in the world, from as far away as South Africa and Japan, are looking to the Canadian model of diversity to design their own programs. While this book is written from a Canadian perspective it is not a Canadian book. Its messages are transferable to any progressive employer.

Chapter 5 will show you how to link diversity with the business strategy. You will examine the case of Ernst and Young and follow the process they have taken to move diversity out of the realm of human resources and into the senior executive boardroom.

Chapter 6 introduces you to one of North America's strongest corporate advocates for diversity as the business case, David Williams, President of National Grocers Co. Ltd. You will read about the barriers he had to overcome in order to obtain commitment from the most senior key opinion leaders in his organization.

Chapters 7, 8, and 9 cover the seven steps to implementing a successful diversity strategy. You will read about fitting the various components together to build an effective program which will lead to evolutionary change. You will read about how to cost an effective program and a detailed implementation schedule is provided to help you to design your own program.

And finally, in Chapter 10 you will be introduced to the fairest in the land. A group of progressive employers who know how to make diversity work. Read about the golden thread that connects them all. What makes them the fairest? What are the initiatives they are pursuing? You will see the best practices being pursued by the best.

The notion of business doing the right thing is usually seen as an oxymoron. People often think that there is some inherent

conflict between reaching the bottom line and making a difference. This book will show you that there is a way to do both.
Diversity at work is a strategy that can work from all perspectives. Diversity at Work leads to fairness—not just for some, but
for all.

Acknowledgements

There are many people who have made this book eminently more readable than it may otherwise have been. A special acknowledgement to Mary Ann Sayers who worked tirelessly on the case studies which form the basis for many of the chapters.

A thank you to all the corporate contacts who participated so willingly and shared their experiences so generously. Special mention to Gerry O'Connor of CASCO, Shelley Pearlman of Ernst and Young, Pam Odam of IBM, Maryann Thornley of London Life, Rob Rochon of National Grocers Co. Ltd., Jan Campbell and Tom Closson of Sunnybrook Health Science Centre, and Maureen Geddes of Union Gas.

My deep appreciation and continued admiration of David Williams, President of National Grocers Co. Ltd.

Thank you to all the excellent professionals at John Wiley & Sons Canada. A special mention to Elizabeth McCurdy (thank you for your patience) and an extra special mention to Karen Milner. Karen, thank you for not giving up!

Finally, I want to acknowledge the two most important people in my life—my son Alexander Wilson, and my life partner, Donnette James. They have both unselfishly sacrificed their time throughout this entire project. Donnette, thank you for your love and your incredible support—especially during the darkest times.

Chapter One

DIVERSITY: THE DEMOGRAPHIC REALITY OF THE WORK FORCE

D iversity is about differences that make a difference—at work and in the marketplace. In particular, how differences between people make a difference in the productivity and effectiveness of an organization. Let us take a quick look at how differences people bring into the world of work can make a difference.

STORIES FROM THE FRONT LINE

Joan is a partner in a large professional firm. She is one of the first women to make it to the partnership level but is now considering leaving. She talks about the realities of being a woman in a male-dominated corporate culture.

"I don't know if it's harder or easier for women in our firm. But I do know I've faced different challenges than those most of my male counterparts have faced. My credibility is frequently questioned by clients who may have outdated attitudes towards women. I am assumed to be either a secretary or junior member of the team in most meetings. Sometimes clients will defer to junior male team members rather than solicit or listen to my perspective. While I have never really faced overt sexual harassment, I've had to put up with inappropriate and sexist remarks made by some of my male teammates. Although I can tolerate them, these remarks diminish my credibility with my clients. The other major concern is the lack of role models to learn from here—not to mention the fact that I will soon face a strong conflict between building a professional career and raising a family."

§

John is a technician in a large manufacturing firm. He talks about the double life he leads as a gay man.

"It is difficult. The first thing you do at work is put out a photograph of your wife and children. If I were to put a photo of my lover and kids on my desk, I would be probably reprimanded for flaunting my sexual orientation.

"First thing on Monday morning, everyone gathers round the coffee machine. 'You went to a movie on Saturday? Oh, who did you go with?' I am forced into lying, staying silent, and looking as if I'm sulking or seeming hostile.

"While I was off work, the people from payroll called and left a message on my home answering machine. Of course the announcement on the machine says you can leave a message for either of us. Next thing I know, it's all round the office: John lives with another man. Now what shall I say?"

§

Lucy is a systems manager for a major financial institution. She talks about the realities of being in a dual-earner family in the nineties. She and her husband have one infant child.

"It's hectic because the child-care centre closes at 6 p.m. and you have to get there on time or face a five-dollars-a-minute penalty. When our son gets sick, things get even more complicated. The daycare won't take the child if he's sick and the sitter that we call for emergencies may not be available. In the past I have split days with my husband working from 6 a.m. until 1 p.m. and I will work from 2 p.m. to 9 p.m. But we can use that type of schedule for only a week. We need more flexibility at work."

§

Jerry is a senior manager in a well-respected insurance company. He talks about the concerns of being the first visible minority in his position.

"Black managers face some challenges that whites just don't. There are few black role models in the company that we can emulate. In turn, white employees may not have a paradigm to help them know what to expect from me. When I was first promoted to this position, there was invariably surprise and sometimes even resistance. Then I experienced the 'employment equity' syndrome, i.e., people assuming I got the job because of my skin colour, not my ability. Frequently I think being as good is simply not good enough. I am always trying to work twice as hard to prove my competence. Many would like to believe that race is no longer an issue. Some argue that this race thing would go away if we simply stopped talking about it. More importantly, senior people in this company are not even comfortable dealing with race-related issues. But we need to start dealing with these issues or people will begin to leave in frustration."

§

Cathy is a nurse in a large urban hospital. She talks about her struggles in caring for her elderly parents.

"Within the past two years, both of my parents have become ill, one with terminal cancer. I have to spend a lot more time with them. Not only am I responsible for ensuring that they are fed and cared for, but I also have to take them to the doctor and therapy appointments. Most time-consuming of all is providing emotional support to my mother as my father's condition deteriorates. I would like to be able to spend more time with them but my work prevents it."

§

Donald is a chemical engineer at a well-known food-processing organization. He barely missed the last down-size in the organization. He talks about his future prospects.

"My days here are clearly numbered. How many other people with grey hair do you see walking around the halls? It's just not part of the corporate uniform. I was going to try to upgrade my skills by finishing my MBA. But why should I? By the time I'd have finished the program, I'd have run out of runway here. I've started to put my attention on the business opportunity I'll take after I get the package. It's too bad, I used to be one of this company's most loyal employees."

§

Carol is a supervisor of a data-processing unit in a large securities firm. Her department includes employees of several different nationalities. She has had a recurring problem dealing with unique management issues when these cultures clash.

"It is difficult keeping harmony in the department. Each culture seems to form cliques. You can see it when you look in the cafeteria at lunch time—the West Indians sit over here, the Portuguese over here, and the Filipinos and East Indians in the other two corners. It's hard to develop a team spirit, especially when most of the time they speak to each other in their mother tongue. Today, for example, Sheena refuses to work beside Mohammed because she claims he put a curse on her. How am I supposed to manage that?"

§

Linda and Alison are the first two females in a large plastics-processing plant. They are contemplating filing a gender harassment complaint against the company for the treatment they have had to face in the workplace.

"At first it was tolerable. Many of the guys settled in to the idea of having women working in the plant. But a small group felt we were invading their turf and had no right to be there. Some of them actually complained that if we were not there they would be getting more overtime. They started to pin nasty drawings of us on the lunch-room bulletin board, they frequently broke into our change rooms, and recently someone broke into my locker and left a pornographic picture. People should not have to work in an environment like this!"

§

Blair is a lawyer in a prestigious corporate law firm. He is recently divorced and has joint custody of two teenage children. He is beginning to realize that his personal values may be out of step with the firm's.

"When I joined the firm I was 25, single, and determined to build a successful career probably at any personal cost. This is one of the reasons my marriage failed. The divorce has totally changed my outlook on life and my priorities, both professional and personal. I am determined to spend a significant amount of time with my children. This would require me working on in-town cases with minimal travel. I'm not sure it is possible to have a full-time career in this firm and be an effective parent, especially a single parent. There is very little tolerance for flexible work arrangements. If your personal priorities do not put work first, then your commitment will get questioned."

§

These are all issues associated with the changing nature of the North American work force. They are examples taken from actual events we have come across in our consulting work in over a decade, as we began to uncover how diversity affects the workplace. There is no reason to think that these events are happening in only some workplaces. It is our experience that issues associated with diversity are occurring in every industry, every region, and every conceivable work environment—including your own.

THE CHANGING DEMOGRAPHIC REALITY

The issue of diversity has arisen largely as a result of some significant changes in the Canadian population and work force. For many years, Canada's society was relatively homogeneous, but as the Canadian population became more diverse, issues of unfair treatment became more evident. Opportunities for racism in the workplace, for example, increase as more racial minorities enter the work force. Likewise, opportunities for sexism increase as the work-force representation moves from an 80-20 to a 50-50 male-female ratio.

It is estimated that white able-bodied males constituted 80 percent of net, new entrants to the labour force from the 1940s to the 1970s. In 1987, a well-respected research organization in the United States gained headlines with a report entitled *Workforce 2000: Work and Workers in the 21st Century*. This report documented some sweeping labour-force changes in the United States and Canada that would substantially affect the way corporations operate in the next millennium. One of the most startling predictions was that white able-bodied males would constitute less than 20 percent of net new entrants to the Canadian labour force over the next decade. This does sound startling but less so when you remember we are talking about a net number. That is, most people leaving the work force will be white able-bodied males while most people entering will be from other groups. The net number of entrants will be the difference between the number of those leaving and the number of those coming in.

OUR CHANGING WORK FORCE

Let us take a look at the composition of the newer entrants to the labour force.

Women

By far the largest group is women, and they are entering the Canadian labour force today at all income levels and almost all ages and occupational classifications. Women are entering at such a rate that by the year 2000 they will represent 50 percent of the Canadian work force. In fact, in some areas of this country, such as Chatham-Windsor, women have already surpassed 50 percent of the work force.

There are several reasons for this demographic trend concerning women. One is the shift in attitudes towards women in the workplace. At the beginning of the century, a woman had very few economic options. She could stay with her parents or get married. If she wanted a job, she was restricted to a few occupations. She could become a teacher, nurse, or domestic worker. As last resorts, she could turn to religion and become a nun or turn to the street and become a prostitute.

Today women are knocking on the door of every occupation. They now represent approximately 50 percent of graduates with degrees in business and management, up from 10 percent in 1970. In the past 20 years in Canada, we have seen dramatic increases in the number of women in every so-called male-dominated field. In computer science the percentage of women is up from 14 percent to 36 percent. In architecture and environmental design, it is up from 12 percent to 36 percent. In protective services (i.e., policing and security), it is up from 9 percent to 37 percent.

Two additional reasons that there are more women in the work force are the effectiveness of birth control and the economic realities of the developed world.

In the developed world, birth control is almost at 100 percent effectiveness, giving women more control over their ability to pursue uninterrupted careers or the choice to wait longer before having children.

In addition, the economic reality in most cities in the developed world is that it is difficult to survive without two full-time salaries. In Canada, dual-earning families are now the norm, with 57 percent of women reporting income from employment outside the home.

More Dual-Earner Families

With more women working outside the home, more mothers and fathers will combine the responsibilities of child raising with the requirements of their jobs. However, Canadian women continue to experience the "double day" phenomenon—employed Canadian women spend approximately twice as much time doing unpaid household chores as their male counterparts. As males take on more responsibility for domestic work within the family home, they are also experiencing difficulty balancing work and family obligations. A 1988 study of more than 6,000 employees at Du Pont showed that 33 percent of men expressed an interest in the part-time option for family reasons. This was almost double the amount of men who favoured that option in 1985.

The work and family demands of dual-earner families may be surpassed by yet another group entering the Canadian work force—the heads of single-parent families.

More Single-Parent Families

Between 1977 and 1984, 163,000 single parents joined the Canadian work force. By 1986, labour-force participation for single parents had reached almost 62 percent. The Vanier Institute of the Family estimates that almost 15 percent of Canadian families are led by single parents. More than 80 percent of these families were mother-led but the institute indicates that the number of father-led single-parent families is on the rise.

More Women with Responsibility for Infant Children

Labour-force participation for women with children under the age of three has risen significantly over the past few years. In 1976, less than 32 percent of mothers with infant children were in the paid work force. Today it is estimated that more than 50 percent of mothers with children under three are in the labour force—with almost 70 percent of them working full time.

The issues for women with infant children are significantly more stressful than for women with teenage children. Unexpected events such as the illness of a child or cancellation of baby-sitters are compounded for mothers of children under the age of three, because they are usually the primary care-giver for the child.

An Older Work Force

The most rapidly growing group in the Canadian work force over the next few years will be workers 45 to 54 years of age. This is because approximately 8 million baby boomers will begin to approach mature adulthood. The median age of the population has increased from 26.2 years in 1971 to 31.1 years by 1985 and is projected to be 37 years by the year 2000.

There is also a trend for both males and females to work longer. Women now spend between 34 and 37 years on average in the paid labour force, a term comparable to men. This drives another trend—more workers with responsibility for the elderly.

More Workers Caring for Elderly Parents or Relatives

Aging baby boomers will not only be the fastest-growing segment of the work force, but they will also be the group sharing much of the responsibility for elderly parents or relatives. It is estimated that 20 percent of Canadians will be over the age of 65 by the year 2021. As Canada's social welfare and health system changes, many more workers will find themselves caring for elderly family members.

Women in the 45-to-54 age category have been dubbed the "sandwich generation." They are women who are sandwiched between two sets of dependants. They have responsibility for children and also the primary care for aging parents. As members of the sandwich generation enter the Canadian work force, issues related to elder care will become more prevalent in the work force.

Today two out of five people 30 years of age and older provide some kind of care for elderly relatives. The Conference Board of Canada estimates that by the year 2000, 77 percent of employees will have some type of responsibility for elder care.

People of Colour and Ethnic Minorities

In the 1950s, 80 percent of immigrants came from Great Britain or Europe. Immigrants from Europe and Britain were given preference for entry into Canada because under the immigration policy these areas were considered preferred-status regions of the world. The proportion of immigrants from the "traditional-source" countries didn't change much in the 1960s, but by the 1970s something began to happen to the composition of immigrants to Canada because of a shift in immigration policy. In the mid-sixties, Canada shifted to a system that required immigrants to score a minimum number of points to gain entry to the country. These points were based on education, skills, ability to speak one of the official languages, financial independence, and other economic criteria. This system disrupted the previous practice of giving arbitrary preference to immigrants from Europe and Britain, and more immigrants began to enter from the Developing World.

By the 1980s almost 85 percent of immigrants arriving in Canada came from countries in the Developing World, changing the racial mix of immigrants arriving in Canada. This trend is expected to continue and in the next 20 years, the racial minority population in Canada will increase from about 6 percent to about 11 percent. If 11 percent does not sound like a huge number, remember that the black population in the United States today is 12 percent.

Many of these immigrants settle in large urban centres, which are now experiencing a racial and cultural mix previously unseen. A large proportion of our immigrants settle in Ontario's urban areas but almost every major metropolitan area in Canada has been and will be affected, as illustrated in Figure 1.1. Every major city will face a doubling, tripling, or in the case of Toronto, a five-fold increase in the racial minority population. Fifty years ago Toronto was predominantly white Anglo-Saxon Protestant. Demographer John Samuels predicts by the year 2000 its population will be almost 50 percent made up of racial minorities. This international city will include every language, culture, and religion found in the world.

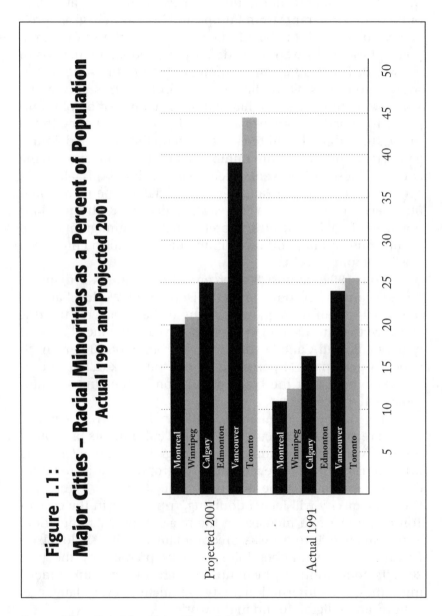

Figure 1.1:

Major Cities – Racial Minorities as a Percent of Population

Actual 1991 and Projected 2001

Source: Canadian Advertising Foundation

People with Disabilities and Employees Caring for People with Disabilities

Another new group entering the Canadian work force over the next decade will be persons with disabilities. This change is driven by two interrelated shifts: attitude and technology.

In the 1950s people with disabilities were removed from society and sent to segregated institutions or sheltered workshops. Spurred on by the victories of the civil rights and women's movements, activists for the disabled have demanded and won the rights for inclusion into mainstream society.

Technology has also changed. Thirty years ago, if you wanted to communicate with someone with a hearing disability, you needed a huge machine that cost well over $10,000. This machine now costs about $300 and has been reduced to the size of a pocket calculator. A few years ago a new piece of technology was invented called the Dragon Dictate machine. This machine could actually scan written material and translate the words into a synthetic voice to allow blind people to read. When it was introduced, it cost well over $20,000. It is about to be overtaken by a smaller, faster, more efficient model that costs a mere $5,000. As the technology rapidly develops, within a couple of years this type of machine will probably be available at the local computer store for less than $100.

While many people with disabilities are able to find employment, a large proportion still do not work. A national study on health and disability showed that out of a working-age population of 2.5 million people with disabilities, only 842,000 were physically independent. Fully 1.1 million were dependent on others; the remaining 558,000 fell somewhere in between, at least partially dependent on others. It is predicted that the number of people combining a job with care-giving for a relative with a disability will also increase.

Gay and Lesbian Workers

It is estimated that 10 percent of the Canadian work force is predominantly gay. It has been difficult to prove this number since many people may not be willing to identify themselves as long as there may be negative repercussions in doing so. Coalitions for

gay and lesbian rights have continued to push the government
to protect and enshrine their human rights. It is likely that all
human rights codes across the country will begin to include sexual orientation as a prohibited ground of discrimination and
harassment. As this happens, it is likely that the workplace will
become more conducive to lesbian and gay workers and they
will feel free to disclose personal information. This could generate several workplace issues associated with homophobia and
inclusionary benefits for same-sex relationships.

Aboriginal People

Another group entering the Canadian work force is aboriginal
people. One-third of aboriginal Canadians are in the pre-labour
force age range today in Canada. Aboriginal communities have
younger populations than the average Canadian population.
This means a disproportionate number of aboriginal people will
become available to work over the next 10 years.

Changing Worker Values

Many corporations are already experiencing a shift in worker
values. This shift is evident as workers demand more autonomy,
challenges, and stimulation on the job. Here again this is affected by the huge number of baby boomers entering higher and
more responsible positions in the organization. These workers
differ from their predecessors, who may have been more willing
to conform, follow out of loyalty, and "sell their soul to the corporation." These "new workers" are more demanding and expect
greater employee involvement, better work and family balance,
and access to more vital information.

THE CONSEQUENCES OF A MORE DIVERSE WORK FORCE

It is clear that the Canadian work force is changing dramatically.
The demographic and labour shifts will significantly affect the way
Canadian organizations function. This is the new reality facing corporations today. What are the consequences for ignoring this reality? There are many and they are all connected to business.

The major consequence of ignoring diversity relates to productivity issues. An organization ignoring diversity can expect to see reduced productivity as workers reduce discretionary effort. This is a highly significant issue in the information age where service-oriented industries will dominate. In such industries the means of production is almost totally controlled by the worker. For example, an insurance agency cannot force its customer-service representatives to offer better service—they must choose to.

Ignoring diversity will also impact on increased competitive costs. Dissatisfied workers are bound to take more sick days off and abuse short- and long-term disability programs. Reducing absenteeism costs continues to be a major concern for North American business. Ignoring diversity could also lead to increased litigation costs due to harassment and discrimination lawsuits. There is a clear pattern of higher financial settlements awarded by human rights commissions across this country.

Another major cost associated with ignoring diversity relates to increased turnover. For years organizations have realized that the dollars used to recruit, select, and train a good employee are lost when that employee leaves. Many organizations are starting to realize that as the economy improves, their most productive workers are leaving to seek opportunities elsewhere. These companies can no longer afford to lose these well-trained people merely because their needs were ignored or they were treated unfairly. This is especially a concern for businesses in high technology industries which are facing an increasing skills shortage.

Another cost of ignoring diversity relates to teams. Many organizations are now moving to a team-based decision-making structure. This requires an increased inter-dependence among employees. Ignoring diversity will inhibit full participation of team members and disrupt the workings of an effective team.

There are as many benefits to embracing diversity as there are consequences for ignoring it and these can occur in both the marketplace and the workplace. In the workplace the benefits are simply the corollary of the situations created by ignoring diversity. It starts with issues surrounding productivity.

An organization acknowledging diversity can expect to create a more supportive work environment that will maximize discretionary employee effort. The most productive workers will find themselves in a highly supportive environment that will be conducive to increased effort and performance. Furthermore, this type of environment will encourage the best employees to stay rather than seek economic opportunities with the competition or elsewhere.

The retention of the best people will directly impact on costs of recruitment, selection, and training. By retaining high-producing employees, an organization can maximize its return on the costs spent on these employees. More importantly, the atmosphere created by valuing diversity will allow all employees an opportunity to maximize their full potential by removing attitudinal and systemic barriers.

Another major benefit to embracing diversity relates to the effectiveness of teams. Organizations come to realize how the concept of diversity becomes a basic component of a strong team. Valuing the differences of each team member will allow the organization to take advantage of a diverse set of skills available in the work force. Capturing these skills and incorporating them in a team will allow a powerful synergy to develop, which will translate into a higher quality of production.

Diversity will also prove to be a major benefit in recruiting people from non-traditional environments. This will allow an organization to access innovative ideas that will contribute to future growth. People from diverse backgrounds will encourage the organization to push past its traditional modes of thinking. Different opinions and perspectives will be highly essential in the new business environment most organizations are now finding themselves in.

As mentioned earlier, the changing nature of the family is a significant demographic reality for all employers today. The old paradigm of family being sacrificed for work and vice-versa is proving obsolete. Acknowledging diversity will allow an organization to create a win/win trade-off between work and family responsibilities. It will allow an organization to develop more flexible work arrangements that will improve productivity as well as the quality of life in the home.

There are also benefits in the marketplace for recognizing the issue of diversity. As an organization begins to reflect the diversity of its marketplace, it is far more likely to be able to relate to its customers' needs. This will allow it to improve the value of goods and services offered to its customers, which will ultimately lead to more sales. An organization can significantly increase market share by ensuring that it reflects the interests of its customers in its work force.

A second benefit is the improved reputation of the business in the marketplace. Organizations valuing diversity will be seen as leaders in their field and in touch with the realities of the changing nature of society. Customers expect their suppliers to be on top of the critical business issues of the day and diversity is clearly one of them. More importantly, customers are more demanding today and will seek out the supplier of choice who has the best intellectual capital available.

A third market benefit relates to globalization. As international trade barriers come down and business attempts to move into unknown markets, having a diverse work force can be a major advantage. Differences in race, culture, language, customs, style, etc., will become an essential consideration for future business opportunities. Acknowledging and valuing diversity will provide the appropriate context for these business opportunities to grow.

It is time business recognizes that a diverse work force and marketplace operates significantly differently than a homogeneous work force. The question is how do we deal with this new diversity?

TIME FOR A NEW HUMAN RESOURCE STRATEGY

The search for the answer begins by looking at the whole question of how we have handled human resources over the past 50 years. Our human resource strategies dictated the way organizations managed people and how they handled differing situations and needs. To understand the various strategies, we can look at three different periods, which we will call the Age of Inequality, the Age of Equality, and the Age of Equity.

The Age of Inequality (1950-1960)

This age represented the twilight of industrialization. North American society was relatively homogeneous and predictable. Families were mostly nuclear and heterosexual, and Christianity was the faith of choice. Divorce, single parenthood, and homosexuality were frowned upon. Differences in race, culture, physical or mental disability, religion, and anything else were noted and responded to, often negatively.

In the workplace, "fit" was important. Most organizations hired people who "fit" the norm. Those who did not "fit" were either not hired or removed. To those seeking employment or promotions, "who you knew" and "who knew you" were far more important than "what you knew." Connections, networks, and the right social circles were clearly the most important elements of the career-planning process. For example, attendance at the right social events organized by the right social club were far more important than pursuing a course at the local university.

The Age of Inequality was also characterized by predictability. People knew the rules and generally followed them. For example, it was assumed that the man was the sole bread winner and the woman stayed home with the kids. It was also common for women to be asked to leave their jobs the moment it was discovered that they were pregnant. Many women actually hid their pregnancies with baggy sweaters in order to get a couple more months of work. In some organizations, the moment a woman was engaged, she was asked to leave the organization. Those who did not follow the rules had to assimilate or leave.

Then came the sixties.

The Age of Equality (1960-1990)

A massive transition occurred during the sixties, prompted by the sexual revolution, the feminist revolution, the civil rights movement, and populist sentiments ignited by the antiwar movement. Everywhere there was a growing consciousness of the lack of equality in North American society. The lack of equality between men and women was taken on by the feminist movement. The lack of equality between whites and non-whites was taken on by the civil rights movement. The lack of equality between the "haves" and "have nots" was highlighted by the peace movement. Change was everywhere, including the work-place.

Managers who were used to seeing their employees as appendages to brute technology were introduced to new management strategies that were more humane. They were urged to ignore the differences that had led to discrimination in the past and to treat all employees equally.

Treating employees equally was clearly a more superior management strategy to the one that existed in the previous age. In the Age of Equality, differences in gender, race, physical or mental disability, sexual orientation, family status, etc., were all ignored. Ignoring the differences was much more equitable than having the differences make a difference. It was also the law. The Age of Equality was also the dawn of human rights legislation. This legislation continued to stress the predictability, desirability, and convenience of treating all employees the same.

But this human resource management strategy also had its shortcomings. In a homogeneous society, where there is a relatively homogeneous set of needs, treating people equally or the same means treating a majority of people fairly. However, as a work force becomes more diverse, a management strategy that stresses treating people the same can lead to inequitable treatment. For example, the RCMP policy that required all officers to wear the same type of hat was found to discriminate against qualified Sikhs merely because they wore turbans.

Much of the inequity in employment systems today occurs because employees are treated the same and differences are ignored. In a diverse work force, when differences are ignored, equal treatment actually causes inequity. In a diverse work force, differences must be acknowledged.

We are on the verge of moving out of the Age of Equality to a new strategy that is consistent with the diverse needs of a diverse work force.

The Age of Equity (2000 +)

The shift into the Age of Equity occurs when organizations begin to acknowledge differences between people instead of ignoring them. This is the goal of a diversity strategy—to recognize and acknowledge differences. This means acknowledging individual employee needs and then accommodating these needs to achieve a more equitable employment system.

Organizations that have made the transition to the Age of Equity accommodate the needs of their employees for reasons other than altruism. Instead, they strive to become the "employer of choice" in their industry. They realize that, as the recession ends, a declining work force and a shortage of skilled labour will force employers to come up with innovative strategies to attract, retain, and utilize the best of their human resources. Any corporation that chooses to ignore its employees' needs—that is, to remain in the Age of Equality—may find itself at a competitive disadvantage. The best members of the work force will seek employers who are cognizant of the demographic changes we have outlined and have begun to respond by pursuing a diversity strategy.

In other words, companies in the Age of Equity actually believe the old axiom "our human resources are our most important assets" and their action proves it. They have begun paying attention to the different needs of their people, not just because it is the right thing to do but because they know it will directly affect the productivity and competitiveness of their business.

It is important to recognize that equality is not equity. Equality means treating people the same and ignoring their differences. Equity means treating people fairly by first acknowledging their differences. In a diverse work force, treating people the same may lead to inequity.

A diversity strategy shifts an organization to the Age of Equity where people get treated fairly, and needs get acknowledged and accommodated. Let us now look at the key components and the goal of a diversity strategy.

The Diversity Strategy

A diversity strategy looks at how differences in
- gender,
- race,
- age,

- culture,
- physical or mental disability,
- sexual orientation,
- nationality,
- religion,
- language,
- class,
- education,
- style,
- personality,
- family status

can and sometimes do affect productivity and effectiveness in the workplace. In this book we will look at the five essential components of an effective diversity strategy:

1. management commitment,
2. employee awareness and understanding,
3. employee involvement,
4. effective measurement,
5. alignment to the business strategy.

We will illustrate these components in action by reviewing actual case studies of corporate leaders in the diversity field. These are organizations that have internalized the business case for diversity and can outline how they are responding to the demographic changes we have discussed so far.

The next two chapters will look at the goal of any diversity strategy—i.e., the creation of an equitable or fair employment system in order to improve the bottom line/business. These chapters will look at the theoretical underpinnings of a fair employment system and how a diverse work force impacts on equitable treatment.

Chapter Two

EQUITY: THE GOAL OF A DIVERSITY STRATEGY

E quity in the workplace has become a highly contentious issue. There is not even agreement about the meaning of the term. Does equity mean correcting past inequities for selected groups, or does it mean creating equity for all groups? Does it mean giving preferential treatment to black men, or removing preferential treatment of white men? Can equity in the workplace be legislated, or is equity impossible unless legislated? Does equity remove white men's unfettered access to economic opportunity, or does it mean white men need not apply?

Many of these questions arise because of various governmental attempts to legislate fairness in the workplace. The United States has affirmative action, which goes back to the civil rights movement in 1961. Canada has legislated employment equity, which goes back to 1984 and a federal government report submitted by Judge Rosalie Abella. Legislated equity clouded the issue of fairness in the workplace by designating certain groups. The government argued that these designated groups disproportionately faced discrimination in the past and now deserved special treatment. Legislated equity was designed to correct the past injustices and create equitable employment for the designated groups. The problem with legislated equity was that it frequently created more inequity by totally ignoring one major group—i.e., white able-bodied males. It was soon clear that legislated equity had very little to do with real equity.

Let us move past the noise created by governments and legislated equity and go back to some basics. Let us begin with the definition of the word "equity." When we talk about equity, we are talking about fairness. The goal of a diversity program is fairness but, unlike the legislated approach, in diversity we are talking about fairness for all.

The goal of a diversity program is to create a fair or equitable employment system for all employees. This is a system that is dominated by merit and fairness. In such a system the best person always gets hired and always gets promoted. Therefore such a system cannot be "fairer" for me as a black male than it can be for a white male. If it is "fairer" for me, then it is not actually fair.

HOW DOES AN EQUITABLE EMPLOYMENT SYSTEM OPERATE?

To understand how an equitable employment system operates, we must use a classic, theoretical management model called Expectancy Theory, which was first postulated in 1968 by two

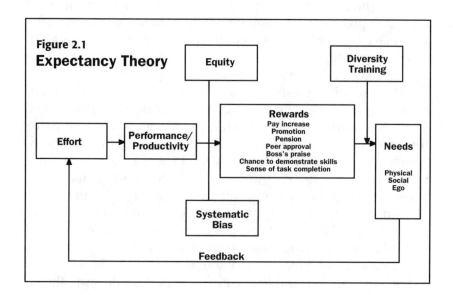

Figure 2.1
Expectancy Theory

economists, George Strauss and Leonard Sayles. Strauss and Sayles were attempting to show the link between effective human resource management and productivity in organizations.

According to the theory, employees will be motivated to produce only if they expect that productivity will lead to a goal they value. More explicitly, increased effort will lead to increased performance or productivity. Increased productivity will lead in turn to rewards that provide satisfaction of important employee needs. A final requirement is that the satisfaction resulting from this initial effort will be sufficiently great to make the effort worthwhile in order for it to continue.

In Figure 2.1 the box marked Equity between Productivity and Rewards represents the employees' perception of the system. If an employee perceives that the system is fair, then he or she assumes that working hard will lead to productivity and he or she will be equitably rewarded. A reward need not be monetary—i.e., a raise or promotion. It could be a pat on the back or a chance to demonstrate another skill or another method of acknowledgement.

Assuming employees perceive the system to be fair, this is the way an equitable employment system works:

high effort→high productivity→high rewards→high satisfaction

If you have an employment system that operates this way, then you have a fair or equitable employment system.

Likewise, you have an equitable system if it operates this way:

low effort→low productivity→low rewards→low satisfaction

In this case, the employee doesn't work very hard and doesn't produce, and you eventually fire him or her. This is also fair. This is equitable. It may not be apparent how this would contribute to higher productivity but it relates to the retention of the best employees. An equitable employment system seeks to attract and retain the highest producers. Thus, those who do not produce will be let go or at the very least not be rewarded. An equitable system is consistent and predictable for every employee.

It will always reward high producers and always punish low producers.

Employees perceive inequity in employment systems for two reasons:

1. Employees perceive that the system treats them unfairly because of their difference. We call this systemic discrimination.

2. Employees feel people in the system treat them unfairly because of their difference. We call this attitudinal discrimination.

In other words, if the fairest people in the world run an unfair system, employees will perceive the system to be inequitable. If the most unfair people in the world run a fair system, the employees will still perceive that the system is inequitable.

Perceived inequity in employment systems disrupts the link between effort, productivity, and rewards.

Let us look at examples of attitudinal and systemic discrimination to demonstrate how inequity disrupts productivity.

Attitudinal Discrimination

Jane's Case

Jane was the first woman ever to work in one of the Acme chain's warehouses. When she was hired, she was told that she was not going to be treated differently from the men and that she would be expected to produce the same amount of work as they.

The average number of boxes moved per day per "man" in the warehouse was 30, and the maximum number of boxes ever moved in the warehouse was 35. Jane was told she would have to work "very, very, hard" to move that number of boxes every day. More importantly ,she was not expected to move that many boxes; she was expected to move the average number of boxes—30.

Jane started her first week at work highly charged. She was determined to prove that her gender made no difference in her ability to perform. By the end of the first week, Jane had distinguished herself as the most productive worker in the warehouse by moving an average of 36 boxes per day, one box more than the previous record. Jane continued this exceptional effort for the first three months.

Management began to send new hires to Jane for training, hoping that some of her new techniques would spread. Jane trained the new entrants even though it meant that her production suffered a bit. She felt that it could give her a chance to move into a supervisory position in the warehouse. In order to protect her productivity record, she came in an hour early for work or stayed a bit later. She assumed the investment would eventually pay off.

A few months later, a supervisory position became available. Jane's application was one of five submitted. The others were from men. Jane was short-listed and was granted an interview. She felt the interview went well, although she was confused when her manager asked about her relationship with her long-time boyfriend. A week later, the new supervisor was announced. Jane didn't get the job. When she asked why, her manager mumbled something about the "guys not yet being ready for a woman supervisor." But then he said, " Look, Jane, off the record, you are the best person for this job, but I can't afford to give you the job and then have you get pregnant on me and leave."

Jane reminded him that she wasn't pregnant.

"But you could get pregnant, especially since you're thinking about marriage. I won't have to worry about that with Joe. It's a business decision, nothing personal. Maybe the next one, Jane."

Jane left the meeting feeling bitter. She applied for the next two promotions and was again unsuccessful. Both successful candidates had been trained by her. She felt the company was being blatantly unfair, especially in light of her past service.

Jane's attitude towards work became increasingly negative. Now instead of arriving at work early, she would come in a couple of minutes late, sometimes as much as half an hour. She also took every allowable sick day off. Then Jane began to sell cosmetics on the side. In the middle of the day, she would leave her work station to make sales calls.

Needless to say, Jane's productivity dropped to an unacceptable rate. Management couldn't understand what was wrong. They were considering putting Jane on probation when she quit. The competition had hired her as supervisor of their warehouse.

Acme thus lost its most productive worker—not its most productive female or designated group worker—but its most productive worker to date. They lost this worker because of perceived inequity in the employment system.

In Jane's case, the employment system looked like this:

high effort→high productivity→low rewards→low satisfaction

Eventually the low satisfaction created by the perceived inequity in the attitudes of the people led to increasingly lower effort and the ultimate low productivity, i.e., turnover.

Systemic Discrimination

Companies usually introduce systems to reduce the type of attitudinal abuses that occurred in Jane's case. Employment systems are designed to treat employees fairly and encourage them to produce. Sometimes, however, systems that were designed to be neutral have a discriminatory effect on employees because of a particular difference. This is called systemic discrimination.

A common example of systemic discrimination would be a company that does not have a ramp entrance or washrooms that are accessible to wheelchair users. Qualified candidates using wheelchairs therefore get excluded from working in a company even though no one has set up a policy to deliberately exclude them.

Seniority and entitlement programs can also systemically discriminate against hiring and promoting the most qualified person. A promotion system based solely on seniority may exclude highly qualified people who are newer to the work force. This concern is generally avoided by the labour movement, which argues that seniority is gender- and race-neutral, therefore it cannot discriminate. But clearly seniority-dominated promotional systems create an artificial bias against those who have fewer years but are more qualified than the next person in line.

A more interesting form of systemic discrimination is preferential treatment for specific groups, sometimes called affirmative action. In this case, the inequity occurs against the most qualified candidates, who may not be members of the preferred group. However, preferential treatment can also create discrimination against the very group it is meant to help.

The Case of Union Gas

Union Gas is a large regulatory energy company in southwestern Ontario. Maureen Geddes is the company's facilitator of workplace diversity. Geddes tells the following story of the company's first foray into preferential treatment for women.

"In 1982 a couple of members of the board of directors expressed concern that they didn't see many women showing up in management. So we started to count. Every year, the vice-president of human resources reported to the Human Resource Committee of the Board of Directors on the number of women in management, supervisory, and technical roles (MST).

"In 1982, 8.2 percent of the roughly 900 MST roles were held by women. By 1992, a decade later, that percentage had increased to 20.5 percent. The increase, however, was at a steadily decreasing rate, to the point where by 1993 we were down to 17.7 percent. The issue was the trend compared to what was available in the labour force at the time. The number of women in the labour force was increasing at a steadily increasing rate over the same time frame. By 1991, according to Statistics Canada, the percentage of women in management and supervisory roles alone was 40 percent. So the question for us became why were proportionately fewer women showing up in management at Union Gas, when they were showing up in steadily increasing numbers at other companies.

"One of our senior executives had taken a particular interest in championing change regarding women in the organization. In the early eighties, he started asking his regional managers to report on the number of women in what we call 'non-traditional' roles. By 1987, 29 of the approximately 900 hourly and technical roles were held by women. Five years later, after repeated hammering by senior management, we were up to ... 29 women. In 1993 the number had actually reduced to 28. What is interesting is that the 28 women in 1993 were not the same 29 women from 1987. Women, for some reason, came in to the organization then left. They went in and out, in and out, sending a signal that something was wrong with the system.

"We hired consultants to conduct focus groups in the organization. They surveyed groups of men and women at various levels throughout the organization from clerical to management. A majority of men and women surveyed expressed concern that the focus on representation statistics had created the perception of affirmative action. The irony was that we have never had a formal affirmative action program at Union Gas. But the highly visible affirmative action moves we made called into question credibility and merit virtually every time a female was appointed. People believed that the fact that you wore a skirt mattered more than the work you did.

"That's when we realized that the perception of fairness of our employment systems mattered more than the number of women at each level. And we threw away the numbers approach. We finally realized that a focus on representation may increase numbers in the short run, but in the long run, you will create an environment that is more hostile to the very group that you want to support. "

Inequitable Affirmative Action

The Union Gas experience shows how the system of preferential treatment can create inequity for both the target as well as the non-designated groups. Today the system of affirmative action is being questioned in the United States by some of the most enlightened social thinkers. The argument is similar to the conclusions reached by Union Gas—i.e., affirmative action actually creates systemic discrimination against those it is designed to help.

Shelby Steele is one of the most vocal activists against affirmative action. In his book, *The Content of Our Character,* he outlines his specific arguments of why he feels the system of affirmative action has shown itself to be more bad than good for the very group that receives the so-called preferential treatment. Steele introduces the concept of "implied inferiority." "What this means in practical terms is that when blacks deliver themselves into integrated situations they encounter a nasty little reflex in whites, a mindless, atavistic reflex that responds to the colour black with negative stereotypes, such as intellectual ineptness."

Shelby goes further to suggest that the individual who benefits from preferred treatment may also be personally affected by "implied inferiority." This may manifest in increased self-doubt and reduced motivation to produce.

If he is right, then this model of inequity may exist:

low effort→low productivity→high rewards→low satisfaction

I can relate to Steele's analysis. I used to work for one of Canada's major chartered banks. I was the worst banker in the history of that bank. I hated banking and never put a lot of effort into it. It never surprised me that my low effort led to low productivity. However, it always surprised me that my low productivity led to promotions. Year after year after year, I got promoted in this bank.

After the third promotion, I started to wonder if they were promoting me because of my performance or because I am black. Given my productivity record, I quickly surmised the bank was under government pressure to promote more minorities and was promoting me because of my race.

After this, I started to reduce my effort further. The reason relates to how my self-esteem related to Steele's concept of implied inferiority. I, just like anyone else, did not want to be promoted solely because of my race. Most people want to be hired and promoted because they deserve the job, because of merit. When you are promoted for reasons unrelated to merit— e.g., tokenism—there is little reason to continue to exert effort. Eventually I left the banking profession, but I still remember the animosity these affirmative action-type moves created among other non-target group workers. What was their motivation to produce?

Employment systems are designed to treat employees fairly in a consistent and predictable manner. When employees perceive that the system is working equitably, they are motivated to exert effort that leads to productivity for an organization. When employees perceive an inequity in the system, their motivation to produce is disrupted and they begin to reduce productivity and may eventually leave the organization.

THE BUSINESS CASE FOR EQUITY

For years leaders of organizations have said that "[their] human resources are [their] most important assets." It is written in annual reports and on company vision statements and is articulated every year at the annual Christmas party. Companies continue to espouse these principles because they think it is better for their business. But how? For example, how does the fair and equitable treatment of people affect the bottom line? Does it make a difference if there is inequity in an employment system?

To understand how inequity can affect a business, let us review the following fictional case study.

The Case of New Era Technology

New Era Technology is a multi-million-dollar computer hardware manufacturing company with operations across Canada. Its manufacturing centres are concentrated primarily in the province of Ontario. New Era is a major contractor to the federal government and employs more than 2,500 people.

The company has divided its revenue producers into three major areas:

• computer hardware manufacturing,

• computer installation, maintenance, and repair, and

• technological upgrading.

Lately, New Era has seen its market share drop significantly in all three categories. An external study of the organization was conducted to determine the reasons behind this trend. The study highlighted a number of possible reasons, including:

• The computer hardware market has become more competitive with a number of new entrants that are challenging New Era's position.

• New Era customers have complained that product quality is dropping in all three areas. Customer complaints are up, as are the number of service calls on recently installed equipment.

• The productivity of the research and development group (as measured by new product launches) has been falling steadily in the last few years.

• Despite recent down-sizing, personnel costs have increased due to overtime and the need for temporary staff to cover absentee employees.

The executive of New Era felt that while the entry of new competitors could account for some of the loss of business, it could not be the sole reason. They knew that the total market was growing, yet New Era had not been able to increase its market share because the company had lost its leadership role in product development and high quality standards.

New Era had already re-engineered the technical aspects of its business—its manufacturing and product development methods. The executive then decided to look at how people-management issues such as management style and employee morale were affecting their problems.

An external consultant conducted a series of focus groups with New Era employees and found the following themes.

• Managers staffed in their own image, offering career development opportunities only to their senior staff.

• Managers were afraid to make mistakes; therefore, they would not allow their best staff to be promoted and would not take risks putting untried people into new positions.

• Alternative work arrangements were extremely rare—employees felt that "face time" (how much time they were physically present in the office) was more important than results. Managers were unclear about how they would manage staff in non-traditional arrangements.

• The procedure for agreeing on non-traditional arrangements was onerous, time-consuming, and discouraging.

• Fully 20 percent of employees had experienced workplace harassment while at New Era.

The consultant offered the following implications for the above findings.

• New Era did not have a good reputation as an employer in its operating communities and thus had problems in recruiting high-calibre talent. As a result, the selection pools for recruitment of skilled workers were limited.

- The lack of career development opportunities for most staff appeared to have stifled the organization's creativity for new product launches.

- A major factor of declining productivity and increased costs was caused by significant increases in short-term disability and absenteeism due to the inability of management to deal with harassment cases quickly and firmly. The legal costs associated with harassment cases at New Era were over $2 million the previous year. By industry standards this was high. It was difficult yet necessary to estimate the additional costs of harassment associated with absenteeism, "on-the-job" absenteeism, and turnover.

It was concluded that New Era leadership begin a process to deal with some of the major human resource issues in the organization and to refocus its goals from process management to creating a system that recruited, employed, and retained the best and brightest in the market.

The New Era case study is based on an actual situation faced by a major Canadian organization today. It gives us an opportunity to see how the fair and equitable treatment of employees can affect the bottom line. How does the creation of equitable systems contribute to the bottom line?

The Model for the Business Case for Equity

To answer this question, we will use a theory that is a modification of a model put forward by Heskett, Jones, Loveman, Sasser, and Schlesinger in a 1994 *Harvard Business Review* article entitled "Putting the Service-Profit Chain to Work." This model will allow us to appreciate why a business may be motivated to pursue fairness in its employment system.

The business case for equity begins with the assumptions inherent in expectancy theory, that is, an equitable employment system will lead to a higher level of employee satisfaction, which will lead to a higher level of employee commitment. We can measure employee commitment in two ways: rates of retention and productivity.

An equitable system is designed to retain the highest-producing employees and weed out the "deadwood." Deadwood

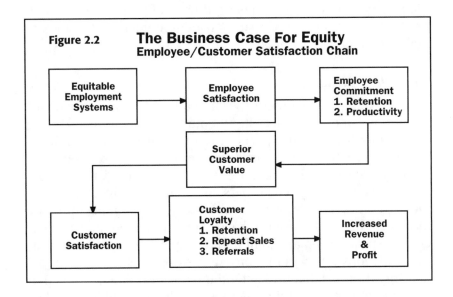

Figure 2.2   The Business Case For Equity
Employee/Customer Satisfaction Chain

will always stay with an organization unless the employment system provides these employees with an incentive to leave. Equitable systems are designed to do this. They punish the lowest producers and reward the highest producers.

If Acme had treated Jane fairly, she would have been unlikely to seek opportunities with its competition. Jane also showed how an employee will reduce her productivity when her needs are not satisfied. Reduced productivity in dissatisfied employees is not immediate. The productivity loss increases as the dissatisfied employee moves from milder forms of effort reductions— e.g., lateness—to more damaging forms—e.g., abuse of short-term disability programs—to the ultimate in reduced effort: termination. Organizations spend millions of dollars every year dealing with the human resource issues associated with absenteeism and turnover.

The next connection in the business case is the link between retaining high-producing employees in order to retain your customers. Organizations using the business case for equity assume that retaining their most productive people will positively affect the quality of customer value. Customer value is becoming a key determinant of how organizations structure their business.

Many organizations are focusing their marketing, service, and production strategies on customer-focused goals. Let us look at how customer value works.

Customer Value

Value is what the customer expects in return for his or her financial outlay. For example, a customer purchases a computer service contract for $1,000 and expects two service visits every year. If the customer gets two service visits every month, the perceived value of the service would increase. Value is simply "bang for the buck."

In this economy, customers are continuously demanding more for less. This is why it's necessary that organizations be more productive. In order to keep up with the demands of their customers and keep ahead of their competition, they must continuously look for ways to increase customer value.

Organizations that understand the business case assume that by attracting and retaining the most productive employees, they can significantly affect customer value. National Grocers/Loblaws president David Williams stands behind their human resource vision statement, which says, "People are the driving force for excellence." In his words, "Any competitor can get our products, our technology or pricing, but no one can get our people. Our people are the key to our competitive edge."

National Grocers, like many other organizations today, recognizes the need to provide superior customer value in a service-oriented economy. They attempt to focus their activities on the needs and expectations of their customers. Williams recognizes that the strength and quality of relationships with the customer will allow the organization to better determine and meet customer expectations. These relationships will be established through individual employees. Thus each individual employee becomes an important link in the achievement of the corporate vision for excellent customer value.

In his book, *Job Shock,* Harry Dent Jr. highlights the case of Hallmark Cards, which restructured its organization around the activities its customers valued. The company found that the key differentiation for card shoppers is the holiday or occasion they are celebrating. So Hallmark reorganized from its traditional differentiation schemes such as demographics and regional cultures to departments specializing in holidays and other experiences.

Hallmark formed small customer cross-functional specialization teams dedicated to each holiday or special occasion. Each team developed an intimate and unique understanding of its particular customer segment and then designed strategies to provide products that met the customers' needs and to focus on those things their customers valued.

These smaller teams at Hallmark function extremely effectively and rely on strong human connections with their customers. The teams are empowered to meet customer needs and change as the marketplace changes. Teams are responsible for providing, without a complicated bureaucracy, a product the customer values. The reliance on the employee to create strong connections with the customer increases the importance of the individual to the organization.

In the industrial age, work was focused on repetitive, predictable functions. In such an environment, employees are relatively interchangeable. In a customer-focused organization, one-to-one human connections cannot be easily duplicated. The value of the employee rests on the relationship created with customers, not just the employee's direct contribution to the bottom line.

It has been estimated that it takes nearly five years for a broker to rebuild customer relationships that can return $1 million per year in commissions to a brokerage house. In this organization the cost of losing a high performer is not just the usual turnover costs of outreach, recruitment, and training. The real cost is the organization not benefiting from what the employee would have produced had he or she not left: a cumulative loss of at least $2.5 million in commissions.

In a service-oriented economy, high-producing employees are those who have a clear understanding of customer expectations. These employees seek to exceed their customers' expectations by ensuring superior quality and customized service in a timely manner. Customers come to expect this from the organization and are willing to pay for it. In other words, this is what they value.

When high-producing employees leave for any reason, they leave with the relationship they have developed with customers. The relationship belongs to the individual employee, not the corporation. Thus losing high-producing employees may mean losing the most direct connection to that which the customer values in the organization.

Customer Value Links to Customer Satisfaction

The next link in the chain is between customer value and improved customer satisfaction. It is reasonable to expect that if a customer is achieving a "bigger bang for the buck" —i.e., superior customer value—then he or she will be more satisfied.

Aetna Life Insurance Company is a leading provider of financial security products and services in Canada. Over the past two years, the company has initiated several programs designed to respond more quickly to the needs of the customer and offer more value-added service. The organization closely measures customer satisfaction every year. In 1995 the company obtained the highest approval rating from customers since it began to survey. Aetna credits much of the improvement in customer perception to its new focus on enhanced customer service in the areas their customers value, such as speed of processing and paying claims. Aetna feels that the attention paid to improving customer value by way of improved service has directly led to increased customer satisfaction.

Customer Satisfaction Links to Customer Loyalty

The next link connects enhanced customer satisfaction with improved customer loyalty. Customer loyalty is an interesting concept. It can be measured by looking at the three Rs: retention, repeat business, and referrals. Retention is holding on to your customers. A satisfied customer is likely to be a loyal customer. A loyal customer is likely to stay with your organization rather than go to the competition. The second R is repeat business. Repeat business postulates that a satisfied customer is more likely to repurchase the same product over a period of time. The first two Rs in customer loyalty say that a more satisfied customer will stay with you and continue to purchase the same goods and services over a long period of time. The final R, referrals, assumes that a more satisfied customer will tell others about her or his positive experience with your organization and recommend future business. The corollary is that dissatisfied customers will share negative experiences about your company and possibly poison the market for future business.

An example of the customer satisfaction-loyalty link can be seen with the Xerox customer satisfaction survey. Every year Xerox surveys its customers to determine their level of satisfaction. The organization usually polls almost half a million customers per year regarding product and service satisfaction. It uses a five-point scale from 5 (high) to 1 (low). The organization has found that a small difference in customer satisfaction can make a significant difference in the level of customer loyalty, especially in retention and repeat sales. Customers giving Xerox 5s were six times more likely to repurchase from Xerox than a customer who reported being only "satisfied." Based on this evidence, Xerox has revamped its customer satisfaction goal to achieve 100 percent 5s every year.

Xerox has also set a customer satisfaction goal of 0 percent of customers reporting a 1 in customer satisfaction. At Xerox, customers that rate the company a 1 have been dubbed "terrorists." These are previously dissatisfied customers who can have a disproportionately negative effect in the marketplace by spreading uncomplimentary information about the company's products and services. The company recognizes that the aggregate effect of one dissatisfied customer can have a much larger effect on future sales than the referrals of a satisfied customer.

The Link Between Customer Loyalty and Increased Revenue/Profit

The final link in the chain is between loyal customers and increased revenue and profit. Many organizations attempt to bring in new customers and increase market share. While this is a worthy aspiration, the real benefit to the bottom line is in keeping loyal customers. A loyal, lifetime customer will have far more impact on the long-term revenue and profit of a company. It is not enough for an organization to get new customers, it must also keep loyal customers if it is to succeed.

In some industries today, keeping customers is a question of survival. The liquor industry is facing substantially declining markets. Since 1981, the sale of alcoholic spirits has declined almost 37 percent due to increased competition from beer and wine, a societal shift to non-alcoholic beverages, and illegal manufacturing and smuggling. The biggest challenge for companies producing alcohol is to keep loyal clients in an increasingly shrinking market. The most aggressive competitors in the market are offering continuous incentives to their loyal customers, such as larger bottles and regular discount pricing.

Other industries are also realizing the importance of the link between lifetime customers and revenue. It has been estimated that the lifetime revenue stream from a loyal pizza eater can be $8,000, a Cadillac owner $332,000, and a corporate purchaser of commercial aircraft billions of dollars. In today's competitive marketplace, it is not enough to get new customers; an organization must continually look for ways to keep its loyal customers if it is to maximize revenue potential and profit. Which brings us back to the beginning: the creation of equitable employment systems.

The business case for equity links the creation of equitable employment systems to improved employee satisfaction, which leads to a higher level of employee productivity through the retention of the best employees. The chain continues by linking highly productive people to superior customer value, which directly leads to improved customer satisfaction. Improved customer satisfaction will result in enhanced customer loyalty, which has a direct positive effect on revenue and profit.

SUMMARY

In this chapter we have explored the concept of equity. Equity simply means fairness. The goal of a diversity program is to create equitable or fair employment systems. We have come to see that these are employment systems based on the merit principle where the best candidate is hired and promoted at all times. When this does not happen, employees perceive inequity in the system. Inequity can occur when the system is unfair or when people in the system are unfair. When perceived inequity is evident, the link between employee effort and productivity is affected. This will lead to a reduction in employee satisfaction, which can affect employee commitment. A reduction in employee commitment has an impact on the quality of customer relationships, which will eventually lead to a negative impact on revenue and profit.

There are several other approaches to the issue of equity in the workplace besides the business case. In the next chapter, we will consider these approaches by looking at the equity continuum.

Chapter Three
THE EQUITY CONTINUUM

T hus far we have discussed the business reasons to pursue issues of fairness in the workplace. We have come to see that issues of fairness can have a significant impact on employee productivity, customer value, and ultimately revenue and profit. But organizations do not usually pursue equity for business reasons; they are usually motivated by something else.

To gain an appreciation for some of the other approaches to the issues of fairness, we will use an instrument called the equity continuum. This continuum rates organizations on a scale of zero to five regarding how they approach issues of equity in the workplace.

The original idea of rating companies on a continuum was included in a book published in 1992 by Felice N. Schwartz entitled *Breaking with Tradition: Women and Work, the New Fact of Life*. Schwartz was the president of an organization called Catalyst, a well-respected research institute concentrating on issues related to women in the workplace.

Schwartz rated organizations on a scale of five increments that measured how they treated their female employees. In the equity continuum, we have gone a bit further. We are rating organizations on how they deal with issues of fairness for all employees. We have labelled Fives in our continuum as equitable employment systems. Schwartz did not bother to label her Fives because she felt it was a utopion state that was impossible to achieve.

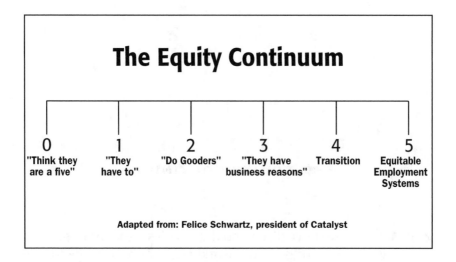

Let us begin the discussion of the continuum by looking at Fives—organizations that have achieved equitable employment systems.

FIVES–EQUITABLE EMPLOYMENT SYSTEMS

At the far end of the continuum are the Fives—organizations that have achieved an equitable employment system. These organizations are dominated by the merit principle, which states that the brightest and best candidate will always get hired and the brightest and best candidate will always get promoted. In these companies, this will happen 100 percent of the time.

Today, there is not one public- or private-sector employer that works this way. Fives are purely mythical, but if they did exist we would call them equitable employment systems. As we said earlier, the goal of a diversity strategy is to create a Five. As an ideal, it may not be reachable in the foreseeable future. The value of setting Five as a goal is to give an appropriate context to any equity activity being pursued and to focus activities in a diversity strategy.

The question is often asked "How do you know when you have achieved a Five?" We will come to see that the answer is "When your employees tell you." Employee perceptions of fairness are critical to the achievement of the goal of a Five.

Zeros — No Problem Here!

At the other end of the continuum are the Zeros. These organizations think they are Fives. When I walk into a Zero to talk about equity, the CEO meets me at the door and says, "Look, there's been a mistake. They shouldn't have called you up here. We don't have any problems. We are one big happy family. We like women here. And women like us. We are a United Nations here. We like minorities here! Now, if you want to talk to one of our minorities, you have to wait because she is making soup in the kitchen right now."

The call of Zeros is "No problem here."

Ones — Legislated Fairness or the Sheriff is on the Corner

Ones approach this issue of equity from a purely legislative perspective. In other words, some law is attempting to make them become fair. In the United States legislated fairness is often referred to as affirmative action. In Canada the usual phrase is mandatory employment equity.

A One would use the following argument to justify pursuing equity initiatives in the organization: "The government is legislating me to be fair to my employees. If I do not comply with this legislation I may face severe fines. The government will see I am complying if I have enough employees from selected designated groups. Let us hire a few of these people so we can get our numbers in line, send a report in, and get the government off our backs!"

We will see that this legislated approach to issues of equity did get some action. We will also see how legislated fairness produced significant issues of white male backlash and tokenism in the United States and Canada. Given the current political environment, we are beginning to see major challenges to legislated fairness programs. Later in this chapter, we will review the demise of a piece of employment equity legislation in the province of Ontario.

Twos — Good Corporate Citizens

Twos on the equity continuum approach these issues from an altruistic perspective. They do it to make themselves feel good. Their distinguishing call is "Let's help these poor people out!"

The argument used in a Two would go like this: "Women, minorities, and other disadvantaged folks have had a pretty tough time over the past 500 years. We are nice people and good people so maybe we should help these poor people out."

When I walk into these organizations, the CEO meets me at the door and says something like, "I'm glad you're here. I would like to introduce you to Betsy, our disabled receptionist. Then we are going to have a tour of our daycare centre. Then we will go through the gymnasium we have for our employees' health. Then we will have a briefing from our EAP (Employee Assistance Program) Co-ordinator. Then we will have lunch with this black guy. We're trying to groom him for senior management and if he keeps his nose clean he could be there in 38 years."

Twos pursue equity issues for altruistic reasons. The goal of a Two is not really to be equitable, but to be good corporate citizens. Its approach is far more piecemeal than an organization that is aiming to be a Five. While a Two may look good because it is pursuing the latest "flavour of the week," employees have long stopped thinking that the leadership is really committed to substantial change. The leader of a Two talks the talk in politically correct terminology without ever thinking that the equity issues are very relevant to the business.

Getting to a Five requires huge organizational change, and a concerted, comprehensive effort of all key opinion leaders in the organization. In a Five, change in attitudes and systems can be and is scientifically measured. In a Two, the only measurement is "keeping up with the Joneses" by monitoring initiatives that benefit selected disadvantaged groups. Even though Twos may look and sound good, they lack the vision and motivation required to achieve real equity in the workplace.

Threes — The Business Reasons

Threes approach the issue of equity because they have significant business reasons to do so. These reasons relate to changes in their competitive marketplace and labour markets due to the demographic shifts outlined in Chapter 1.

A Three has set the vision of becoming a Five but has not begun to take action on it. It has, however, made a substantial philosophical shift on the issue by seeing it as a legitimate business issue rather than legislative (like a One) or altruistic (like a Two). As we saw in the last chapter, the leaders of a Three recognize that equity issues can have a significant effect on their productivity, competitiveness, customer service, and revenue generation.

Most Threes are also motivated to pursue equity issues because of some significant labour market changes in North America. These organizations recognize that the North American population and work force will grow more slowly because of a decrease in the fertility rates. In Canada, fertility rates have dropped to 1.6 children per family, lower than the replacement rate for the population. This will tighten labour markets and increase labour shortages in those industries that will be essential to economic development in the Information Age.

Shortages of skilled labour are expected in several industries in North America as we approach the new millenium. Some of these industries, such as computer software development, are already discovering that finding and keeping the best employees is difficult even when unemployment rates are high. This is because of a gap between the skills of available labour and the required skills for the more "knowledge-based" occupations of the information age. Close to 60 percent of organizations surveyed in the Workforce 2000 Study conducted by the Hudson Institute reported difficulty in hiring technical, managerial, and professional employees. For these companies, not attracting the most qualified employees or losing the best employees to the competition has become a very costly proposition.

Threes assume that talent is evenly distributed among all

genders, races, and cultures. Thus their approach to equity is more inclusive than either the Ones or Twos. They have set the vision of getting to a Five for everyone in their employment system, including white able-bodied males. In a Three, issues of tokenism and reverse discrimination are unlikely to be relevant.

Threes also measure the achievement of fairness differently. A One would say the organization is fair when it has enough members of various designated groups employed throughout the organization. A Three would say that representation numbers could be used as signals that inequity may exist but the real test for equity is the proper measurement of employees' attitudes.

Fours — Transition

Fours are organizations that have acknowledged the business case to equity and have now started, in Schwartz's words, to level the playing field. These organizations have begun to actively remove systemic and attitudinal barriers that stand in the way of operating an employment system based solely on merit and fairness.

Fours are attempting to remove these barriers by ridding their employment systems of systemic bias, educating their employees about attitudinal bias, and valuing and managing diversity.

Fives — Still Only a Goal

In our consulting practice at TWI, we have dealt with hundreds of organizations pursuing equity initiatives. In our experience, we have found no organizations that would fall between a Four and a Five on the equity continuum. We would say that less than 0.1 percent would be between a Three and a Four. Approximately 20 percent would be between a Two and a Three. Thirty percent would rate between a One and a Two. The remaining almost 50 percent of organizations would be between a Zero and a One.

One of the major reasons that organizations do not see the business side of equity is because of the impact of legislated fairness programs. Whenever and wherever government has entered the conversation about equity in the workplace, the key arguments relating to the business case have been missed. Let us make a quick review of the history of legislated fairness and identify the critical events that clouded the real issues of equity in the workplace.

A BRIEF HISTORY OF LEGISLATED FAIRNESS IN THE UNITED STATES AND CANADA

1961

To understand how the government became involved in legislating fairness we must go back to the civil rights activities of the early sixties. On March 6, 1961, President John F. Kennedy signed Executive Order 10925, which established the President's Commission on Equal Employment Opportunity and a contract compliance requirement for businesses providing goods and services to the U.S. government.

This order stated, "The contractor will take affirmative action to ensure that applicants are employed, and employees are treated during their employment without [emphsis added] regard to their race, creed, color, or national origin." It is important to recognize that the executive order did not call for preferential treatment for any group. It merely continued the traditional goals of nondiscrimination in hiring that had been pursued as far back as 1941 by President Roosevelt towards defence contractors.

1964

In 1964 the *Civil Rights Act* was passed by the U.S. Congress. Title VII of the act not only prohibits an employer from discriminating because of race, colour, religion, sex, or national origin, it also specifically states that the act is not designed to "grant preferential treatment to any group." This language was deliberate to ensure that the act could pass the Senate, which was influenced by several strong representatives from the South.

One of the sponsors of the bill, Senator Joseph Clark, ensured Title VII was interpreted correctly when he stated emphatically during the Senate debate, "There is no requirement in Title VII that an employer maintain a racial balance in his work force. On the contrary, any deliberate attempt to maintain a racial balance, whatever such a balance may be, would involve a violation of Title VII, because maintaining such a balance would require an employer to hire or to refuse to hire on the basis of race."

1965

The first time any indication of preferential treatment occured in any government pronouncement was during a speech made by President Lyndon Johnson in June 1965. Johnson told his mostly black audience at Howard University, "You do not take a person who, for years, has been hobbled by chains and liberate him, bring him to the starting line of a race and then say 'You are free to compete with all others' and still justly believe you have been completely fair."

This speech began to reshape the affirmative action debate in the United States and affected the issue of legislated fairness for years to come. After this, non-discrimination as a passive activity no longer met the requirements of any government pursuing legislated fairness. By the time the Johnson administration ended, government contractors were expected to come up with hiring plans that resulted in minority employees being added to their work force. The government had clearly shifted into a more aggressive enforcement mode regarding issues of affirmative action.

1968

In 1968 another milestone occurred for federal contractors with the introduction of written affirmative action plans for federal contractors that included the provision of numerical targets. The new regulations declared, "The contractor's program shall provide in detail specific steps to guarantee equal employment opportunity keyed to the problems and needs of minority groups, including, when there are deficiencies, the development of specific goals and timetables for the prompt achievement of full and equal employment opportunity."

The introduction of numerical targets as the means to evaluate the effectiveness of an affirmative action program would again dramatically affect the future of legislated fairness for years to come. Even though the definition of a satisfactory goal was vague, the shift to a numbers perspective was clear. Since 1968, governments have routinely assumed that the purpose of any legislated fairness program should be to correct a past injustice by improving the employment representation of specific groups. The focus on the numbers became and continues to be a preoccupation of advocates for legislated intervention in the field of fairness.

1969

By 1969 the notion of measuring progress by representation had become an accepted practice in the U.S. government. The Nixon administration carried the importance of numbers one step further by introducing hiring quotas for construction companies in a highly controversial initiative known as the Philadelphia Plan. This plan became the model for future government quotas in affirmative action. Within a year, all government contractors with 50 or more employees were required to submit "specific goals and timetables" based on the percentage of the available minority work force or face a loss of their government contract. One critic of this development, Harvard sociologist Nathan Glazer, described this shift as "changing the focus of civil rights from equality of opportunity to racial statistical parity." Even a previous undersecretary of labor to Nixon observed in a *Wall Street Journal* op-ed piece, "Our use of numerical standards in pursuit of equal opportunity has ineluctably led to the very quotas guaranteeing equal results that we initially wished to avoid."

1972

In 1972 two companies—Sears and AT & T—were taken to the Supreme Court by the Equal Employment Opportunity Commission. Both were accused of discriminating against women and minorities. The basis of the government's argument was that both companies did not have a proper representation of women and minorities in senior positions. AT & T lost its case and was required to pay $15 million in back pay to 13,000 women and 2,000 minority men. Sears, however, won the case by using the perception of employees in attitude surveys to prove that women and minorities did not perceive any more discrimination in the Sears' employment system than white males did. The Sears' case was one of the first times representation numbers as an appropriate measurement for equitable treatment were ever successfully challenged in the U.S. judicial system.

1978

In 1978 the Supreme Court struck down the University of California's affirmative action plan in the case of *Regents of the University of*

California v Bakke. The university was forced to admit a white medical school applicant who claimed discrimination under Title VII of the Civil Rights Act of 1964—the same legislation at the root of affirmative action. The court held that the university had set an "impermissible quota" by reserving 16 places for disadvantaged students. The tide against the numbers approach was clearly turning.

1980

In 1980 presidential candidate Ronald Reagan promised in the following statement to halt affirmative action: "We must not allow the noble concept of equal opportunity to be distorted into federal quotas which require race, ethnicity, or sex—rather than ability and qualifications—to be the principal factor in hiring or education." Reagan also appointed Clarence Thomas, a vocal opponent of quotas, to chair the Equal Employment Opportunity Commission. Thomas began a concerted effort to reduce the reliance on numerical representation as the primary focus of affirmative action programs. His argument was that the reliance on quotas was a "weak and limited weapon" against inequity in the workplace. The numbers, in Thomas's perspective, distorted the real issues surrounding discrimination. In his words, "This policy fails because it allows an employer to hide continuing discrimination behind good numbers."

This notion of the numbers being the wrong focus of legislated equity began the debate on the effectiveness of affirmative action that continues today. While it is clear that numerical representation is no longer considered an effective solution to inequity in the workplace, the debate has yet to identify an effective alternative.

1984

Canada's foray into legislated equity began in 1984 with the Royal Commission on Equality in Employment chaired by Judge Rosalie Abella. Unlike in the United States, the Canadian commission moved immediately to preferential attention for four groups: women, racial minorities, persons with disabilities, and aboriginal people. According to the commission, individuals from these four groups experienced "restricted employment opportunities, limited access to decision-making and little recognition as contributing Canadians." The commission coined the phrase "employment equity," which was described as a "strategy to obliterate the present and residual effects of discrimination" facing the so-called four designated groups. The commission called on the Canadian government to introduce strong and specific employment equity legislation. Inherent in the commission's recommendations was the assumption that numerical representation was the proper evaluation tool to determine when equity in the workplace was achieved.

1986

In 1986 the federal government introduced Canada's first *Employment Equity Act*. The act incorporated many of the recommendations of the Abella commission, including the designation of four disadvantaged groups and the reliance on numerical representation as the primary means of evaluating progress. This new law applied to approximately 370 federally regulated employers and approximately 900 companies that provided goods and services to the federal government. It was estimated that the act would have an impact on a work force of more than 1.5 million employees.

The anti-quota debate in the United States was not entirely lost on the Canadian legislators. An attempt was made to distinguish U.S. style quotas from more reasonable Canadian-style goals and timetables. The difference, according to the government, was that quotas were rigid, externally imposed numbers while goals and timetables were flexible, internally generated numbers. The subtle difference was missed by many critics of legislated equity programs who cautioned about following the model created in the United States.

1991

In October 1991 the Special Committee on the Review of the Federal *Employment Equity Act* was established. The mandate of this committee was to undertake a comprehensive review of the provisions and operations of the act and submit a report by May 1992. A further review was conducted by the Canadian Human

Rights Commission and various other advocacy groups, including the Urban Alliance of Race Relations and even the Conference Board of Canada.

All reviews indicated the same thing—statistical improvement for employment representation for designated groups was extremely slow. In approximately five years, representation for women and racial minorities had increased by only 3 percent. The percentage of aboriginals and persons with disabilities employed represented less than 4 percent of the work force, far fewer than data would imply are available.

More importantly, the reviews highlighted the now-familiar U.S. debate regarding the appropriateness of numerical representation as the primary determinant of success. Business spoke of the amount of time and money wasted in administering the system to track the numbers instead of pursuing longer term equity initiatives. The Conference Board reported that less than 10 percent of employment equity budgets was spent on actual equity programs. The vast majority of these equity budgets went into salaries and systems to collect the numerical data to complete the onerous government reports.

Even the most ardent activists for legislated equity began questioning the effectiveness of the numbers approach. Laurie Beachell, the national co-ordinator of the Coalition of Provincial Organizations of the Handicapped, was severely critical of the federal act. In a review of the act, he is quoted as saying, "The act as it was passed was doomed to fail because it amounted to little more than merely mandatory reporting of data. In and of itself, data will do little to improve the status of disadvantaged sectors."

1992

Early in 1992 the Ontario provincial government began consultations on introducing mandatory employment equity legislation for the province of Ontario. Under consideration: how should numbers be set? Not under consideration: should numbers be used? Under consideration: which definitions should be used for designated groups? Not under consideration: should there be preferred status for groups?

A group by the name of the Business Consortium on Employment Equity, representing a diverse group of employers with more than 56,000 employees, urged the government to move past the moral and social perspective on equity and pay heed to the economic and business vantage point. The consortium also warned the government to entrench the merit principle in the legislation and avoid the pitfalls of reverse discrimination and tokenism inherent in quota-driven programs.

The group strongly advocated the use of other mechanisms besides numerical reprsentation to determine progress. In a submission to the Office of the Employment Equity Commissioner, the consortium stated, "We also note the need for qualitative measures to reflect cultural change within an organization which may also indicate the achievement of a more equitable workplace. This point reflects the concern that the achievement of equity be measured by qualitative as well as quantitative change within an organization. Qualitative change may be measured by using vehicles such as attitude surveys, focus groups or sample environmental scans of the organization."

A few months later the Ontario government introduced mandatory employment equity legislation for the province of Ontario. The preamble to the bill was mute on issues of merit, business realities, and qualitative measurement. Instead the focus was clearly on the under-representation of the same designated groups in "most areas of employment, especially in senior and management positions." The major purpose of the bill was to improve the numerical representation of selected groups in the work force.

1993

By this time in the United States the debate on affirmative action had reached a fever pitch. A national debate on hiring quotas was precipitated by a number of Supreme Court decisions against affirmative action programs, the Bush administration veto of a civil rights bill, and the resentments caused by group preferences.

The *Harvard Business Review* published a controversial paper entitled "The Forgotten White Male," featuring an academic study that showed that white males were becoming less attached and committed to the workplace as affirmative action programs took hold. The covers of national magazines, among them *Business Week*, screamed headlines such as "Does Affirmative Action Work?" and "Backlash-Debating Affirmative Action." These publications began to ask questions surrounding merit in hiring, race-based preferences, tokenism, white male backlash, and the age-old question of reliance on numerical representation.

In Canada, the federal government continued on its established path. The government of Ontario ran into unexpected resistance on its own employment equity initiatives. It ran an advertisement for a senior position in a ministry office that stated that consideration would be limited to candidates from the four designated groups. The conservative press in Ontario went wild. Headlines such as "White Males Need Not Apply" confirmed the worst fears of critics of legislated fairness. The ad was eventually withdrawn but the damage had been done.

1995

The debate on affirmative action in the United States continued, gaining steam every month. *Newsweek* ran a provocative cover story entitled "Affirmative Action: When Preferences Work — And Don't!" Affirmative action was pronounced as the new wedge issue in American life destined to become a major campaign platform for the Republican right wing. The magazine conducted its own poll, which indicated that 75 percent of Americans think that qualified blacks should not receive preference over equally qualified whites in getting into college or getting jobs. In California the Civil Rights Initiative was introduced, which would bar any form of affirmative action preference based on race, gender, ethnicity, and national origin for state hiring, contracting, or education.

Ontario found itself in the middle of a provincial election as the debate in the United States raged on. The employment equity law was barely a year old and the Employment Equity Commission was not even fully established. It was at this time that the Progressive Conservative Party gambled with an election ploy that could have backfired if not picked up by the electorate. The party vowed to kill the new employment equity law on the grounds that it was quota-driven, ignored the merit principle, and advocated preferential hiring. The genius of the Conservative ploy was that it capitalized on the anti-affirmative action sentiment dominating the airwaves controlled by U.S. media. It also exploited the confusion that existed between quotas and goals and timetables.

By election night on June 8, 1995, it was clear that the gamble had paid off. The Progressive Conservatives were swept into office with a huge majority and a mandate to pursue all promises. Within a month of its election, the new goverment announced it would make good on its promise to repeal legislated employment equity before the end of the year. The social experiment had been killed before it had even started.

BUSINESS TO THE RESCUE — A RETURN TO DIVERSITY

Two weeks after the election, my previous consulting company, Omnibus, conducted a survey of more than 200 organizations in Ontario, many of which had been pursuing diversity programs. We wanted to determine the impact repealing the employment equity bill would have on these companies pursuing equity and diversity initiatives. Fully 70 percent of respondents indicated that they had made some progress towards equity within their organizations. Seventy percent of these organizations also indicated that the change or repeal of the employment equity law would have little or no impact on their plans. Less than 8 percent of respondents indicated they would cease initiatives because of the new government's intentions.

An article in the spring 1995 publication *Canadian Business Review* may explain the Omnibus survey. The article was entitled "Building a Business Case for Diversity." It distinguished between the basic tenets of diversity and legislated employment equity, the former being an inclusive concept for all employees, not just preferred groups, and most importantly pursued on a voluntary basis as a strategic business response to changing demographics. While legislated employment equity was about numerical representation, diversity was measured differently. Diversity avoided all the concerns raised by legislated equity programs since they began more than 30 years ago.

The article said; "Forward thinking Canadian organizations have recognized that competing successfully in the new global marketplace requires more than the lastest technology, most efficient production processes, or most innovative products. Canadian organizations' competitive strength is increasingly contingent on human resources. Competing to win in the global economy will require an ability to attract, retain, motivate and develop high-potential employees of both genders from a variety of cultural and ethnic backgrounds. The challenge facing today's corporate leaders is to foster an organizational culture that values differences and maximizes the potential of all employees. In other words, leaders must learn to manage diversity."

In short, diversity had become the business case for equity. Organizations commited to diversity are actually Threes—they have business reasons to pursue equity that go beyond legislative and political mandates.

Let us now take a look at how these organizations are pursuing and implementing diversity initiatives without the requirements of government legislation.

Chapter Four

THE ESSENTIAL COMPONENTS OF A DIVERSITY STRATEGY

What can we learn from more than 30 years' experience of legislated fairness in North America? What are the characteristics of a legislated program that eventually causes it to self-destruct? By reviewing the lessons learned from the demise of legislated fairness, we can better understand the essential components of a successful diversity strategy.

Four important lessons can be learned from the legislated fairness experiences. They are:

1. A diversity strategy must be linked to a business objective, not for the social and moral purpose of correcting past injustices.

2. A diversity strategy cannot result in preferential treatment for some groups. It must be inclusive of all employees.

3. A diversity strategy must protect the merit principle to avoid tokenism and reverse discrimination.

4. A diversity strategy is not simply based on the numerical representation of an internal work force reflecting the external available work force.

Let us look at each lesson in turn.

LESSON 1: LINK DIVERSITY STRATEGIES TO BUSINESS OBJECTIVES

One of the clearest lessons learned from the history of legislated fairness is the need to find the right motivation for a diversity program. The motivation for a legislated program stemmed from the belief that there was a need to correct past injustices towards selected groups. In other words, the reasons for the program were either social or altruistic.

Corporate philanthropy and good citizenship are most effective during prosperous times because companies can afford to spend time and resources to help the downtrodden and less fortunate when their own house is in order. As well, during good times, when corporate profits may be high, these good citizenship programs can provide effective tax benefits and improve a company's public image.

When times are less prosperous, corporations are not as likely to see altruism as a high priority. During highly competitive and tough times, the business agenda is dominated by concerns such as maintaining and increasing market share, improving productivity, increasing revenues, reducing costs, and making profits. Any thought of helping the less fortunate is unlikely to come before the corporation's concern about helping itself.

We know that many corporations are in the middle of the most challenging competitive period since the Industrial Revolution. Globalization is opening every market to increased competition. Customers have become more demanding and informed. Technology is easily duplicated and changing at a rapid pace. In order for organizations to survive the transition to the Information Age, they must concentrate all their resources on finding the secret to sustainable competitive advantage.

Legislated fairness programs failed to recognize the business realities corporations face today. Governments assumed they could either force corporations to be fair or rely on "white male guilt" to generate effective programs once inequity was identified. These assumptions were clearly misguided.

Forcing an organization to be fair sometimes leads to a sophisticated manipulation of the process. There are several cases of this in the U.S. experience, one of which involved a fire department that until 1978 had employed no blacks. In 1978 the department adopted a policy of reserving a number of positions exclusively for black firefighters as an affirmative action measure. The department held to this quota and even went so far as to replace blacks who left with other blacks, and whites with other whites, presumably under the impression that this was what was meant by equal opportunity. Behind the numbers, however, was continued discrimination against blacks. The black firefighters hired under the program were subjected to racial harassment and generally did not advance within the department. One black firefighter, who resigned after four years, said that blacks knew they were there "because they need a quota." The policy, far from eliminating consideration of race in the workplace, actually encouraged the inequitable treatment of blacks but technically met the government's affirmative action requirements.

In other words, forcing the organization to be fair actually encouraged discriminatory treatment. This organization had figured out a way to use the system of affirmative action to continue business as usual. There are also times when some organizations used the loopholes of the affirmative action system to their own advantage. In these cases, blacks or women were set up as puppet presidents to front organizations in order to get government contracts because of "set-asides" for minority contractors. As is the case with many laws, organizations eventually found loopholes in legislated equity programs to serve their purpose, but totally distort the original objective of the law.

There is no reason to think that the same thing was not happening in Canada. In a 1994 report entitled *Equity at Work*, the Canadian Human Rights Commission laments the number of employers who have attempted to sabotage the government process through lengthy court challenges and procedural questions. The Commission even claims the federal government was guilty of this. The report states: "Probably the most disappointing feature of this program to date has been the fact that the public sector has failed to lead the way. Given what should have been the Government's commitment to its own legislation, this is surprising to say the least of it. The powers that be have regrettably appeared more preoccupied with pausing long and hard on bureaucratic detail or disputing the Commission's role than with making substantial progress."

Why Do Legislated Programs Fail to Motivate Organizations to Pursue Effective Equity Programs?

The cause of the failure of legislated fairness programs to motivate employers to pursue effective programs is their inability to show benefit to the employer. In light of the significant business concerns evident today, the secret behind having an effective diversity program is to link the objectives of the program to the key business objectives of the organization. There are at least two ways this can be done:

1. links to the work force,
2. links to the marketplace.

The Work-Force Link

Organizations today are continually searching for ways to ensure sustainable competitive advantage. One approach to competitive advantage is by providing comparable buyer value more efficiently than competitors—i.e. by reduced costs. Automation can be a temporary answer to this but it will not be sustainable because technology is easily duplicated by competition. Witness the video camera and video recorder. Both were invented by Americans but their production is now monopolized by the Japanese, who copied the technology and then improved it to create higher-quality goods more cheaply.

A much more sustainable resource for competitive advantage is human capital or people. It is far more difficult for an organization's competition to duplicate a highly skilled work force. Human resources can become the major leverage for sustainable competitive advantage if managed effectively.

There is some evidence to suggest that Canada needs to improve its management of human capital. Perhaps the most scathing criticism came from one of the world's greatest experts on competitive advantage, Harvard Business School professor Michael Porter. In a 1991 paper prepared for the federal government entitled "Canada at the Cross-roads," Porter indicated that unless Canada cleans up its act in this area, it would be in significant trouble in the competitive world marketplace.

Porter appears to be right. Every year a Swiss-based research body, the World Economic Forum, rates the top 48 competitive countries in the world. Between 1989 and 1994, Canada went from fourth place to sixteenth place in competitiveness. Undoubtedly Canada needs to look for ways to improve its productivity and competitiveness.

One of the major concerns seems to be Canada's inability to effectively utilize all its human resources. For example, Canada ranks eighteenth in Gross Domestic Product per employed person, far behind countries such as Switzerland, Japan, and the United States. Some suggest this is because Canada has an overqualified, under-used work force. This would appear to be the case for at least one segment of the work force—visible minorities.

According to 1991 census data, visible minorities are more likely to have a university degree than others in Canadian society (25 percent vs. 17 percent overall) but fewer are employed in higher paying professional or managerial jobs. Statistics Canada reports that 39 percent of visible minorities with university degrees have managerial jobs. The percentage of whites with university degrees holding managers' jobs is more than 70 percent. While 52 percent of whites with university degrees hold professional positions, less than 13 percent of visible minorities with degrees hold such positions. The report also found that visible minorities with post-secondary or university degrees hold more manual-labour jobs than the control group. In some visible minority populations, such as Southeast Asians, as many as 25 percent of workers with post-secondary education were in manual-labour jobs.

This means that individuals who could be contributing more to the competitive performance of corporations and the economic development of the country are being under-utilized. In 1989, the Ontario government enquired into this issue by sponsoring a study entitled "Access." This two-year study examined the under-utilization of foreign-trained professionals and trades people in the Ontario work force. The government had estimated that the province lost approximately $2 billion a year in productivity by under-employing foreign-trained workers. After a full examination that included more than 200 briefs from various stakeholder groups, the study concluded: "The participants come from many different cultural, educational, economic, professional and non-professional backgrounds. At least half, however, have a trade or profession acquired from the country of origin. Despite this apparent advantage to enter the Canadian work force, we have found that they are just as employment disadvantaged as an immigrant with no marketable skills."

In other words, because the province is not determining the transferable skills of these immigrants, their skills are being totally wasted in the work force. If we factor in the racial minority composition of most new immigrants to Canada—more than 80 percent are people of colour—we can better understand the underemployment statistics for visible minorities mentioned above.

One possible business link for a diversity strategy is to determine how the under-utilization of people may affect the organization's productivity and efficiency. We will come to see how organizations are using a diversity strategy to maximize the utilization of all human resources to improve their bottom line.

Links to the Marketplace

Another possible business motivation to pursue diversity is changes in the domestic or international marketplace. Companies are beginning to recognize that cultural competencies are required as their marketplace changes. Some organizations have begun to capitalize on these changes by shifting their marketing and international business strategies.

In 1993 the Canadian Advertising Foundation sponsored a project designed to examine how the changing nature of the Canadian marketplace would affect the advertising industry. More than 600 companies were surveyed to assess their awareness of diversity issues and the implications for the industry. The study predicted that by the year 2001, the visible minority population in Canada will represent more than 17 percent of the population or almost 6 million people. It also predicted that visible minorities will control about 20 percent of the total national GDP (or about $311 billion) by 2001. These predictions caused many in the advertising industry to shift their perspective on the issue of diversity. The study encouraged the foundation to do more research into how the portrayal of visible minorities in advertising would affect consumer behaviour.

As a follow-up, focus groups were conducted. They found that more than 50 percent of visible minorities surveyed felt using visible minorities in ads made the ad more believable and would affect their purchase of goods and services. The report concluded that "if a company is reflecting the spectrum of the Canadian population in its advertising it can be perceived as saying 'we value all Canadians as customers'—result: more sales." Seventy-seven percent of senior management within companies agreed that ads that feature a good mix of visible minorities and whites are more effective from a business perspective.

Another report enquiring into this issue was produced by the Conference Board of Canada in April 1995; it was called "Dimensions of Diversity in Canadian Business." This report looked at how the changing face of the Canadian consumer has begun to affect the implementation of diversity programs in Canadian organizations. According to the report, "Today, many customer-focused Canadian organizations have recognized the need to incorporate the element of ethno-cultural diversity into their marketing/sales/customer service strategies." Fully 71 percent of survey participants reported that the cultural make-up of their customer base is being used as an important element of their overall marketing and sales strategy.

Sun Life Assurance Co. of Canada is a pioneer in the area of ethno cultural marketing. In 1988 the president of Sun Life, John R. Gardner, made a speech at the Montebello Conference Centre in Quebec about selling to Canada's booming ethnic market. Gardner described Sun Life's Scarborough branch office, which was staffed by a highly diverse multicultural, multiracial group. It included 26 percent WASP, 23 percent Chinese, 23 percent Indo-Pakistani, 15 percent Filipino, 6 percent Italian, and 4 percent

West Indian. The office roughly represented the ethno cultural breakdown of the surrounding area.

Gardner boasted, "Let me put the performance of that ethnic mix into perspective: Scarborough Branch generated roughly $20 million in premium income last year. That was better than the premium income taken in by one-third of the Canadian life insurance companies. Twenty entire companies, not branches but companies, didn't take in as much money as one of our branches did in that year."

Sun Life started to realize that they could substantially increase their revenues by ensuring that they were attractive to the customers they were attempting to serve. They looked at ways of making their customers more comfortable and providing services that their customers valued. They found that by having sales and marketing representatives who were in sync with the various elements of the surrounding markets they could tap new opportunities.

The Sun Life argument can also be made for organizations pursuing new markets internationally. Some of Canada's largest exporters are beginning to take advantage of Canada's ethno-cultural diversity to develop international markets. Canadian Occidental Petroleum Ltd. is one of them. The company's president and CEO, Bernard Isautier, says, "The presence of different ethnic groups is a strong asset for Canada and Canadian business. I firmly believe that if business leaders use the tremendous potential represented by Canada's ethno-cultural groups, Canada will have a much better chance to penetrate emerging global markets."

Significant business issues in their workplace and marketplace will provide organizations with a much stronger motivation to continue an effective diversity strategy than a program dominated by legal, social, and moral imperatives. Attempts to convince organizations that they should pay for the injustices of the past will prove shallow and, as we have seen, are doomed to fail. The secret to the long-term motivation for a diversity strategy is to link it with one of the significant business needs of the organization. In the next chapter, we will review a case study of an organization that has successfully made the link between diversity and its business.

LESSON 2: A DIVERSITY STRATEGY MUST BE INCLUSIVE FOR ALL EMPLOYEES

A second lesson from the history of legislated fairness is the need to include all employees in a diversity program. Governments are frequently driven by political agendas. Most pieces of legislation related to fairness were driven by advocacy groups who fought for the recognition of their particular issues. During the consultations for the Ontario legislation, several groups called for recognition by requesting inclusion as a designated group.

The Coalition for Gay and Lesbian Rights was one of the groups that lobbied the government for inclusion. In a brief entitled "We Count," the group stated, "Lesbians and gay men are not included among the designated groups in the federal employment equity legislation. We look to the government of Ontario to provide leadership to the country by passing employment equity legislation which does not discriminate among minorities. *All Ontarians* must have the opportunity to work on an equal footing and to contribute to Ontario's growth and prosperity."

In its response, the Ontario government acknowledged the high degree of homophobia in the workplace and the "insurmountable barriers" gay men and lesbians face in the world of work. Yet the acknowledged inequities faced by gay men and lesbians were not serious enough to warrant their inclusion as a designated group in the legislation. The government took the same paradoxical approach with other groups that had lobbied for inclusion such as seniors, youth, third-language minorities, and francophones. Why?

Part of the answer rests in the government's reliance on statistical representation in the work force. The government indicated that statistics on the degree of under-representation of these other groups were unavailable. Therefore even though it was clear that all these groups face significant discrimination in employment systems, the government could not prove it by way of numbers.

But there is a more significant reason that the four designated groups (women, visible minorities, aboriginal people, and people with disabilities) were chosen and not others, and it has to do with simple politics. In politics, the squeaky wheel gets the oil. Governments are run by politicians and politicians are motivated by political agendas. The reality is that the four designated groups had put the most pressure on the government over the past decade on the issue of employment equity. Other than the feeble-numbers defence, there is no real consistent rationale to justify keeping other groups out.

But let us return to an important point made by all the aspiring designated groups. It can be seen in the above quotation by the gay and lesbian advocacy group. They maintain the need for equal footing for "all Ontarians." Yet if you pushed these groups, you would find that this was less than genuine. This actually means "all Ontarians except white, able-bodied, heterosexual males." Throughout the government consultation process, there was strong consensus that white able-bodied males should not be covered by the legislation. This is evident from the preamble of the Ontario legislation, which states, "The people of Ontario recognize that Aboriginal people, people with disabilities, members of racial minorities, and women experience higher rates of unemployment than 'other people' in Ontario. The people of Ontario also recognize that people in these groups experience more discrimination than 'other people' in finding employment, in retaining employment and in being promoted. As a result, they are underrepresented in most areas of employment, especially in senior and management positions and they are overrepresented in those areas of employment that provide low pay and little chance for advancement. The burden imposed on the people in the groups and on the communities in which they live is unacceptable."

This preamble allows us to understand the potential for white male backlash in all legislated equity programs. The arbitrary distinction between "people in these groups" begged the question "compared to whom"—i.e., who were these unidentified "other people"? The answer was always the same: white able-bodied males. What is unsaid in this preamble and underlies the thinking of every legislated equity program in North America so far is that white able-bodied males have received unfettered access to economic opportunity for the past century on the backs of disadvantaged groups, and now it is time to turn the tables.

The problem with this "tit for tat" logic is the inability to explain how two wrongs now make a right. If discrimination against my black son was wrong in 1940, how can discrimination against my neighbour's white son be right today? Discrimination is discrimination regardless of the sex, colour, gender, sexual orientation, class, or creed of the perpetrator or the victim. In order to create fairness in society, all discrimination must be attacked.

The name of my previous company, Omnibus, is Latin for "all of us" or "all inclusive." We attempted to remove inequities in employment systems for all groups, not just arbitrarily defined designated groups. This means an Omnibus program includes white able-bodied males. It is interesting to note the amount of criticism our company got for taking this stand.

On December 12, 1994, the *Toronto Star* ran an article entitled "Path to equal workplace not just black or white." It outlined some of the various approaches to issues of fairness in the workplace, including the Omnibus approach. Antoni Shelton, executive director of a highly respected advocacy group called the Urban Alliance on Race Relations, is quoted as saying, "I don't know how Omnibus can justify doing it this way. They talk about all the diversity issues, white men's parenting needs and so on. But there is a huge difference between them and the needs of people of colour, their problems and the barriers that exist to their getting in and staying in the work force."

Is there a huge difference? Does it not depend on who is being asked or who is facing the discrimination? Obviously, the representatives of the Coalition for Gay and Lesbian Rights will feel that their inequities are more relevant than the issues facing visible minorities. Advocacy groups representing women will feel the discrimination they face is more pressing than the discrimination being faced by seniors. Every group can make a case for the removal of its particular inequity. But it is essential that organizations not follow the government's mistake of determining one group's inequity more important than anothers. The way around this is to design inclusive programs.

Women-in-Management Programs

Many organizations make the common mistake of being exclusionary in the design of their equity programs. They start by establishing programs to look exclusively at women in management or issues associated with women in the work force. The rationale for choosing this group over any other is that women represent more than 50 percent of the work force and most of us are either men or women. This is a shaky rationale, to say the least.

What usually happens is the organization appoints a "representative" committee made up of women from throughout the organization. This group's mandate is to ferret out inequities women are facing within the organization and make recommendations to a predominantly male executive. The committee gathers information regarding the issues women are facing by talking to other women in the organization.

The traditional response to the announcement of this committee is predictably negative from both men and women in the organization. Women are usually resentful that the organization has developed a "special program" for them that casts doubt on their ability to succeed. Men are resentful because they feel they are being discriminated against because of the limited mandate of the committee.

The committee responds to this backlash by indicating that the mandate for the committee goes wider than just issues related to women. They will say that many of the initiatives recommended by the committee will also benefit men in the organization—e.g., balancing work and family. The organization also indicates that once the major issues related to women have been handled, the program will be extended to look at the specific inequities facing the other groups. Inevitably this extension never seems to occur and the committee's focus continues to be exclusive. As we saw in the Union Gas case, eventually this initiative designed to support women actually poisons the environment for them.

The Inclusive Approach

After attempting the "women-only" approach for a few years, many organizations eventually realize that instead of looking for reasons to defend the exclusionary approach, they gain greater acceptance by abandoning it for a more inclusive approach. An inclusive approach looks at all forms of discrimination and does not predetermine the importance of one group over the other. In an upcoming chapter, we will review a case study to show how an organization can make inclusiveness an essential element of the diversity program.

LESSON 3: PROTECT THE MERIT PRINCIPLE

One of the most important lessons to be learned from legislated equity programs is the need to protect the merit principle in hiring, promotion, and downsizing. The merit principle has been endemic in the North American work ethic. It underlies the basic belief that if you work hard, you will be rewarded for your efforts.

Senator Jesse Helms, an ultra-conservative critic of U.S. affirmative action, has said that legislated fairness programs "fly in the face of the merit-based society envisioned by the Founding Fathers." Helms fails to observe that the founding fathers were probably envisioning a society that was merit-based for people who looked and acted like them. Merit-based decisions for women and blacks during the founding fathers' age was less realistic or even desirable.

This is not to say we are much better today. We are still envisioning this elusive merit-based society. Thus when people like Senator Helms talk about going back to a merit-based society, we must first acknowledge that we have probably never had one to go back to.

Employment systems are probably fairer today than they were in the past, but how far have we come? How many systems consistently and predictably hire and promote based on merit? That is, how many employment systems really do operate as meritocracies? As we saw earlier with the equity continuum, probably very few. There are all sorts of reasons that most systems don't operate with merit. These inequities routinely prevent the best or most qualified candidate from getting the job.

I remember listening to one woman, whose husband was employed on a police force, who was deeply disturbed about the government's legislated equity program. She felt it gave an unfair advantage to the designated groups over her white able-bodied husband. I asked her if she thought the employment system of the police force had operated based on the merit principle before the legislated equity initiative. She laughed and began to explain that if you did not serve in the right district of the city, if you did not have the right degree from the right school, and if you did not have a well-known family name, you had no chance of being promoted. It turned out her husband had none of these things, and she felt the equity program was going to add even more discrimination to an already unfair system. Now her husband would also lose out on jobs in competition against less qualified designated group candidates.

This was the underlying fear created by the legislated equity program—less qualified designated group candidates would receive promotions over more qualified white candidates. Some of this fear comes from the very nature of the equity debate and some of the labels used to identify the various players. The groups designated under legislated equity programs are frequently referred to as "disadvantaged." This could mean disadvantaged in education, income, social status, or even intelligence. The label of "disadvantaged" creates the impression that somehow these groups can't succeed unless they have help from a special program.

This is what Shelby Steele has labelled "implied inferiority." Listen to how it is manifested in this story told by a law clerk recounting his experiences in law school: "Those of us who have graduated from professional school over the past 15 to 20 years and are not white travel a career path that is frequently bumpy with suspicions that we did not earn the right to be where we are. We bristle when others raise what might be called the affirmative action question—Did you get into a school because of a special program? That prickly sensitivity reveals a rarely mentioned cost of racial preferences. The cost I have in mind is to the psyches of the beneficiaries themselves..."

This "implied inferiority" also happens in Canada. I remember having a conversation with a blue-collar West Indian father who had worked hard to ensure all his kids went to university. One of his sons had worked extremely hard and graduated on the honour roll in computer science. He was immediately offered lucrative employment opportunities with several prospective employers, including the federal government, which happened to have an employment equity program. His father had advised him to take the federal government offer because it would be a secure position. The son took his father's advice and accepted the government job in Ottawa. On the first day of work, he was approached by a veteran of the computer department who asked him, "How does it feel to get a job just because of your skin colour?" The son was confused and bitter. He had worked hard for four years to achieve his results and now his accomplishments were suspect because of the employment equity program.

"Implied inferiority" breeds what some have called the new racism. It is a racism created by the preferential treatment of legislated equity programs. This new racism assumes that members of the disadvantaged groups are not up to the regular standards. Charles Murray, a columnist with *The New Republic*, writes, "The old racism has always openly held that blacks are permanently less competent than whites. The new racism tacitly accepts that, in the course of overcoming the legacy of the old racism, blacks are temporarily less competent than whites. It is an extremely fine distinction. As time goes on, fine distinctions tend to be lost. Preferential treatment is providing persuasive evidence for the old racists, and we can already hear it sotto voce: 'we gave you your chance, we let you educate them and push them into jobs they couldn't have got on their own and coddle them in every way you could. And see: they still aren't as good as whites and you are beginning to admit it yourselves'."

The way to avoid the perils of the new racism and implied inferiority is to engrain deeply the merit principle in any diversity program. To understand how to do this, let us explore the logic of the merit principle.

Defining Merit

We like to describe a meritocracy as an employment system that "maximizes neurons per salary dollar." That is, the neurons or brain cells in my head are the same colour as the neurons in the head of Stephen Hawking. If we could get an organization to look past the packaging of the neurons—i.e., my black body and his wheelchair—then their hiring would be based on merit and maximizing neurons per salary dollar.

Most organizations do not hire this way. It is highly likely that my skin colour, his wheelchair, Maryanne's gender, Jawad's religion, Bruce's age, Carol's family status, Hazel's accent, and any other irrelevant factor will get in the way of merit. Hiring based on merit is about getting past these irrelevant factors and looking only at the information that is relevant to the job search.

There are two sides to what we call the merit equation.

An assessment of the skills necessary to do a particular job + Ability to do the job = MERIT.

The first part of the equation is an assessment of the skills necessary to do a particular job. Most job descriptions do not accurately reflect the transferable skills necessary to do a job. This is because jobs change and the description may not be updated, or the job description may be written for another purpose—e.g., to roughly determine the salary range.

Most employees will find there are many things they do that are not accurately reflected in a job description. The first step in identifying merit is to accurately assess all the necessary skills required to do the job.

The second part of the merit equation is an objective assessment of the candidate's ability to do the job. This requires tests that often may not be administered in the average employment system. It is a far more time-consuming process than many organizations would be willing to take.

One retailer we have worked for has designed an elaborate process to determine employee skills. The organization has surveyed customers, managers, and district directors to determine the characteristics of an outstanding customer service representative. The retailer identified more than 200 specific skills that such a person would possess. The recruitment process begins with the candidate writing a test that determines if he or she has these skills. Successful candidates move to the next step, two four-person panel interviews. The third and final step is a test on the technology the retailer uses for inventory.

Although this process cannot guarantee the best candidate for the job, it is far more scientific than the processes that are more common in employment systems. Usually organizations hire using "who-you-know" referral systems or rely on soft skills such as good communications skills or fit to corporate environments. These soft skills are harder to define and thus are likely to be improperly assessed.

A meritocracy attempts to link the defined transferable skills of a candidate with the required skills of a particular job without regard to irrelevant characteristics such as race, gender, culture, etc. This can be done only if the organization has first ensured that the qualifications for the job have been described accurately in terms of the essential duties to be performed and not in terms of easy screening criteria. While a process dedicated to merit may take longer, it will also allow organizations to find and keep their best employees.

Legislated fairness programs sometimes encouraged employers to consider characteristics unrelated to merit as the deciding factor in the employment decision. This has led to issues of "implied inferiority" and the new racism, which we will discuss later. It is important that these lessons be kept in mind when diversity programs are being designed. The protection and explicit articulation of the merit principle is essential to an effective program. It is also important to avoid the backlash that is created by perceived preferential treatment. We will come to see how effective diversity programs ensure that the merit principle gets protected.

LESSON 4: DON'T RELY ON THE NUMBERS

One of the most important lessons to be learned from the history of legislated fairness is that a program must not rely on numerical representation of the diversity of a work force to measure the success of a program. When the government encouraged organizations to look at the numbers, it inadvertently diverted the attention from the real equity issues.

Clarence Thomas writes about this phenomenon in recounting his early experiences as chair of the Equal Employment Opportunity Commission. "One of the first things I noticed when I came to the Commission was that often it was the employer who pushed for the use of numerical goals in a settlement agreement. Employers seek such a resolution even before the Commission has shown that it can identify actual victims. The reason for this is obvious. In those cases where numerical relief is possible–that is, where there has been a pattern or practice of discrimination affecting a large class—every identified victim has a right to 'make whole' relief. Giving back pay to each actual victim can be quite expensive, but the cost of agreeing to hire a certain number of blacks or women is generally diminishing.... Goals and timetables are easy on employers who want to avoid back pay liability and easy on interest groups that are more concerned with advancing group interests than with the rights of particular individuals. Unfortunately, the use of numerical goals is tough on those actual victims of discrimination who are never identified or compensated and on those victims down the line for whom filling a quota never quite adds up to truly equal opportunity."

In other words, concentrating on the numbers is an easy but ineffective approach to discrimination in the workplace. The traditional focus on the numbers allowed the government to articulate the targets that were required to achieve compliance under the legislation. The problem is that achieving these numerical targets may have had little to do with reducing discrimination or achieving fairness in the employment system.

The government's assumption has always been that if discrimination is removed, an internal work force will mirror the availability of the external work force. This assumption may or may not reflect the reality. We have visited several government departments that have achieved a far more diverse representation of staff than the availability statistics would suggest is possible in spite of the fact that they have done little to remove actual discrimination. Removing discrimination, as Thomas points out, is far more difficult and time-consuming than setting a numerical target. It also requires more organizational commitment.

There are three reasons that organizations succumb to the temptation to use numbers to measure success.

1. Numbers are tangible.

2. The number-setting process does not require major organizational change.

3. Organizations have no other way to measure progress.

Let us take a quick look at each reason.

Numbers Are Tangible Evidence

Organizations measure anything that is important to them. The organization determines a starting point and the method by which ongoing progress will be measured. This type of measurement works effectively for more traditional business areas such as revenue and budget projections. Taking measurements clearly identifies a tangible result that organizations can hold employees accountable for achieving. Unfortunately, this model is less effective when dealing with issues of fair treatment.

As we have seen with the legislative model, focusing on the numbers distorts the real issues of equity. Managers see achieving the numbers as the preponderant goal of the program and pay little attention to anything else. The numbers become the end instead of the means to an end.

In many cases, the tangible nature of numerical representation actually becomes the problem. When managers are urged to focus on the achievement of a specific number, the resources that could be used to identify and reduce discriminatory practices are re-routed to data-collection activities, which can be time-consuming and misdirected. Managers assume that their primary objective is the achievement of the number. This narrow focus frequently encourages them to pursue tokenism and ineffective hiring in order to meet set objectives. The consequences can be far more damaging than any previous discrimination.

The Number-Setting Process Does Not Require Major Change

Organizations that have been under legislated equity programs for many years will admit that the number-setting process is usually relatively unobtrusive. In most cases, a junior manager responsible for compliance performs an analysis of internal representation compared to data for external work force availability. The manager then sets a series of numbers that will be acceptable to the government. A report is filed and not usually looked at again unless the company is audited.

It is unlikely that the senior executive group ever has to be bothered with the process except during the annual briefing. At this time, the junior manager is required to present progress on the numbers and justify why the numbers have not changed. It is at this point that problems usually occur, because it is unlikely that representation numbers change unless something else in the organization has changed. No one individual, including the manager of the equity program, has the power to effect this change alone. But the manager of the equity program is usually accountable for the numbers.

I remember watching one poor employment equity manager being raked over the coals by a senior executive group in a federally regulated organization. The manager was reporting on the numbers that had been set a year earlier and was attempting to provide some rationale for why the organization had not met any of the goals. The executive was furious at the manager and began to suggest that, because the numbers were not met, she had not done her job. The manager explained that it takes a lot more than setting goals and timetables to change an organization's employment process.

Even when management takes responsibility for numerical goals, major organizational change is unlikely. The following case study comes from a 1991 edition of *Business Week* magazine that focused on race issues in the workplace. It highlights the experience of one U.S. federal contractor, Monsanto Chemical Co.

Monsanto is a manufacturer of chemicals and drugs in St. Louis. Boosting the number of minorities and women in its traditionally white male chemicals subsidiary has been a priority at Monsanto since the 1970s. In 1990 17 percent of non-union new hires were minorities; almost 30 percent were women. But women and minorities were also quietly leaving Monsanto at a disproportionate rate. In 1988, 21 percent of employees who voluntarily left were women, while 14 percent were minorities. By 1990, however, the percentages of women and minorities quitting had jumped to 26 percent and 20 percent respectively. Management had discovered that simply dictating numbers in hiring cannot change a corporate culture. One Monsanto manager admitted, "In the 1970s, we had lower expectations for minorities. There was a lot of pressure to keep the numbers up to meet our affirmative action targets so very poor performers were carried. That kind of coddling erects a barrier with other workers—a hell of a barrier."

Monsanto realized that it would have to go beyond the numbers if it were to make organizational change. It would be necessary to use some other form of measurement in its program. This brings us to the third reason organizations use the numbers—the organization lacks any other way to measure progress.

No Other Way to Measure Progress

As we have seen, since 1965 representation numbers have been the primary vehicle to measure progress. The logic for the use of numbers is that they allow an objective measurement of change in the employment process. This logic can be seen in the following quotation from a senior bureaucrat of the Canadian federal government, Gail Stinson, director of Legislated Employment Equity. "You cannot remedy a problem that you cannot measure and that you do not know you have. Employment equity was designed to motivate employers to change their policies and procedures by encouraging them to recognize for themselves that a problem existed. Employers, seeing the actual numbers for the first time, would recognize the degree of under-representation of the designated groups in their organizations and would be encouraged to devise solutions for the problem."

That was the logic behind the reason for using numbers as the focus of legislated equity. Unfortunately, we have seen that merely forcing organizations to collect and analyze numbers leads to little change in employment systems. This is not to say that numbers are irrelevant to the process of introducing fairness into employment systems. Numbers can be used as a kind of oil-light warning to signal inequity, but they are only signals.

Numbers Are the Oil Light

Representation numbers can be used as an "oil light" to indicate inequity may exist in an employment system. That is, they can be rough signals that something has gone wrong with the system. Let us illustrate by looking at Figure 4.1 on the following page.

Diagram A in Figure 4.1 represents the number of people available for work in the census area of Metropolis. Let us assume that this city has an unemployment rate of 10 percent.

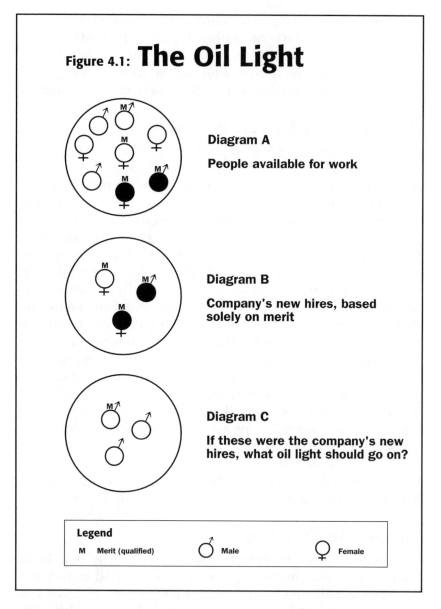

Some of the people unemployed are men, some are women, and a few are racial minorities. There is a new company in Metropolis looking for staff. But not just any staff. This company wants only the most qualified people available in Metropolis. It defines most qualified by the "M" qualification. As we can see from

Diagram A, not all candidates available in the city will be qualified. In fact, only four are—a white woman, a black man, a black
woman, and a white man. If the company hires based solely on
merit, it should hire the staff represented in Diagram B. Notice
that the qualified white male is left out, but not because of his
race or gender qualifications. He has simply been left out
because the company cannot afford to hire all qualified candidates available.

Let us assume that instead of hiring this staff, the company
hires as illustrated in Diagram C. What oil light should go on for
us here? What signal should occur about the way this company
recruited? What is wrong with this picture? It is clear it did not
hire based on merit. It did not hire the most qualified people
because two of the three candidates do not have the qualifications the company was looking for.

Why would somebody do that? Why would a company hire a
majority of candidates who were not qualified when it had
already stated publicly that it wanted to hire only the best candidates? There are many answers to that question but you will
find that all of them rest in one of two subsets—attitudinal or
systemic discrimination. Let us look at some examples.

The obvious example of attitudinal discrimination is that the
company's recruiter had a personal bias against women and
racial minorities. Let's say the company recruiter was Archie
Bunker, who said, "I'll be damned if I'm going to hire a woman
or racial minority and I don't care how qualified they are!" This
could account for the discrepancy in the diagram. While this
scenario is possible, it is not very probable. We don't meet many
major employers with overt racist and sexist recruitment policies
that exhibit this form of intentional discrimination. We do come
across a great deal more subtle discrimination. For example, in
one organization we worked for it was impossible to get a job
unless you played recreational golf or hockey. The organization
based its hiring decisions on the sport the candidate played
instead of on merit. In another organization, hiring was based
on the club the applicant belonged to. In 1960, if you were not a
Shriner or a Mason, it was impossible to get a job in this company.

There are many other examples. If you hire based on a strong
referral system, you will bring in many people like your original

work force because human beings usually surround themselves with people a lot like themselves. If your company uses an ineffective test–that is, a test that is not testing for the skill required on a given job–this could be a barrier. Perhaps the most interesting excuse used is the blame-the-victim attitude many companies use when they declare the minority or female applicants "just won't apply."

One organization was located on the border of an aboriginal reserve. For years, native people had applied to this company for jobs, and for years none were hired because people in the company had prejudice towards the aboriginal people on the reserves. After about 50 years, the aboriginal people stopped applying for advertised positions in the company because they knew the exercise was futile. Then the company started doing business with the federal government. When the company was audited by the government, it was asked why it had not hired more aboriginal people. The company thought that was a good idea and for two years attempted to hire from the reserve. For two years not one native person applied. The company phoned the government back and declared, "They just won't apply." When the government contacted the reserve to see what the problem was, the native people asked if the government had forgotten about the 50-year history the company had in the area. The company ended up producing radio and television ads specifically for the reserve to convince the aboriginal people that the last 50 years were history and that the company really was now interested in hiring them.

Figure 4.2 on the following page lists some of the more common forms of attitudinal and systemic discrimination that could turn the oil light on. Systemic discrimination is far easier to identify and remove. But either form of inequity could affect the representation of any group with merit.

There are hundreds of reasons that the oil light could go on but it's definitely a signal that something has gone wrong. Like the oil light, unbalanced representation numbers are a signal that something may be wrong but they cannot tell the whole story.

To find out what has really gone wrong with the employment system, you have to go past the numbers and measure something else. You have to find a way to measure the perceptions of existing

Figure 4.2

Discrimination

Intentional (Attitudes)	Unintentional (Systems)
Sexism	Seniority
Racism	Entitlement
Ageism	Inflexible Systems
"Haleism" (bias against people with disabilities)	Referral Systems (Who you know)
Creedism	Old Boys' Network
Credentialism	New Girls' Network
Nationalism	Non-Bona Fide Job Requirements
Homophobia	Biased Tests and Interviews
Nepotism	Limited Advertising
Favouritism	Unfair Communications Systems
Classism	Corporate Culture "Fit"
Maternalism	
Paternalism	
Protectionism	

and prospective employees. For example, I have a client that has searched the two top universities in southwestern Ontario to find computer graduates. Over the past 10 years, these two universities have attracted a high percentage of visible-minority students. In fact, more than 60 percent of computer graduates from these institutions are people of colour, the vast majority being Asian. The company has hired 10 to 15 of these universities' graduates every year for the past five years. In that period of time, it has hired only one racial-minority student. The oil light should definitely come on in this case. The representation numbers were very unbalanced in this company: there was a far lower proportion of visible minorities in their work force than were available and qualified in their geographic area. You are saying either that within the 60 percent of graduates who are racial minorities none are the best or that there is something wrong with the employment system. The oil light did come on for this company and it hired Omnibus to review its employment systems. When we asked staff how people got hired, they told us about nepotism and "who you know" recruitment; they perceived that popular jocks on campus were sought out as candidates. The representation numbers had only identified that there might be a problem, but could not identify what was wrong in this employment system.

But how does an organization measure the real issues that are not revealed by the numbers? How can an organization measure unfair attitudes related to gender, race, age, biased selection processes, and other soft variables? We will come to see that effective measurement is at the heart of an effective diversity program.

SUMMARY

The experiments in legislated fairness throughout North America have provided us with some valuable lessons for the design of effective diversity programs. We have learned that an effective diversity strategy must

- be integrated with the business,

- be supported by senior management,

- be inclusive of all employees,

- protect the merit principle,

- not rely solely on numerical representation for measurement.

In the next five chapters we will be examining case studies of organizations that have learned from the history of legislated fairness. We will see how these organizations have used these five key components in order to avoid the mistakes made by government attempts at fairness.

Chapter Five

LINKING THE DIVERSITY STRATEGY TO THE BUSINESS STRATEGY

I n the last chapter we identified the importance of finding the right motivation to initiate a proper diversity strategy. We have seen how legislated fairness programs rely on either fear or altruism to generate movement. We have also seen that such movement will be short-term and minimal. However, programs that are linked to specific business issues will be far more effective and have a much better chance of surviving in the long run.

In this chapter we will concentrate on how to create the link between the diversity strategy and the business plan. We will look at two cases.

Ernst & Young is a leading professional-services firm that provides services to businesses in a wide variety of areas including accounting, auditing, management consulting, and tax planning. This firm began to focus on diversity issues approximately four years ago, linking its program to work-force issues. The organization has incorporated its diversity strategy into its strategic plan and has appointed a director of diversity with responsibility for overseeing the strategy.

The other case study is the Canadian Imperial Bank of Commerce. This organization has linked its diversity strategy with changing marketplace issues. The motivation again goes well past the legislative requirements of the bank's federal employment equity requirements.

LINKING THE DIVERSITY STRATEGY

There are three steps in linking the diversity strategy to the business plan.

1. Establish the key business objectives.

2. Establish relevant diversity issues.

3. Identify the links between the business objectives and the diversity issues.

   Let us review how Ernst & Young worked through each step.

STEP 1: ESTABLISHING THE KEY BUSINESS OBJECTIVES

In August 1993 Ernst & Young produced a strategic plan, which would carry it into the next millennium. In fact, the plan was called Mission Millennium. Ron Gage, Chief Executive Officer of the firm, stated that this plan would chart the course the organization would take as the accounting industry went through a period of great "turbulence, transition and opportunity." Ernst & Young intended to use this period to shift the focus of the entire firm to concentrate on those issues that would allow it to maximize the business opportunities arising from these changes in the industry.

   The basic shift for the organization was to move from growth and diversification to profitability and service integration. The organization recognized that by focusing on profits, it could make the necessary investments in people and technology to guarantee a sustainable competitive advantage in the industry. By concentrating on service integration, the firm could provide superior value to its clients and thus strengthen the long-term client relationship, which would again benefit its competitive position.

Ernst & Young (E&Y) has been guided by two specific values for over a century. These values shape every activity in the firm and guide what takes priority in the business agenda. The two values are clients first and professional excellence. The new strategic plan continued to stress these values but added three others that would also serve as the foundation of the firm. These new values dealt directly with E&Y's principal asset, its human resources. The new values were teamwork, recognition and reward, and openness.

The value related to teamwork was fundamental to integrating the wide range of services the firm offered clients. The organization recognized that in order to provide its clients with the best business solutions, employees had to work more interdependently. This was a shift from the independence mentality that pervades most professional firms.

The firm added recognition and reward as a value to ensure that employees understood that performance would be the basis for reward. This value underscored the firm's desire to retrench merit as the primary driver for the compensation and promotion process.

The value of openness was meant to send a clear message to E&Y people that open communication would be vital to the future success of the firm. An organization that specializes in information had to work to freely share information in order to provide the integrated response that was now being demanded by clients.

Adding the three new values was more than a symbolic gesture. Like other professional firms, E&Y had always put the interests of clients before anything else. While the client continued to be a key focus in the new strategic plan, the addition of the three values clearly signalled the organization's intention to publicly recognize that their employees are also a very important asset. It's clear that E&Y spends more on human capital than any other resource. These new values were meant to create an environment that could be supportive of these assets to ensure they could do the best possible work for their clients.

The Six Business Objectives

To put these values into effect, the firm created six business objectives that were to become the "pillars" of Ernst & Young's strategic focus for the year 2000. By achieving these six objectives, the organization would meet its vision of becoming the leading, most innovative, integrated professional services firm in the market.

These business objectives are:

1. To anticipate client expectations.

2. To develop our people.

3. To integrate our services.

4. To achieve superior profitability.

5. To be innovative and to effectively deploy technology and information.

6. To achieve a prominent market position.

We will come to see how the organization linked these objectives with the emerging diversity issues in their industry.

STEP 2: IDENTIFYING THE RELEVANT DIVERSITY ISSUES

In 1993 the American Institute of Certified Public Accountants (AICPA) conducted a nation-wide survey of public accounting firms. The focus of the survey was to determine the status of women at all levels within the public accounting industry. The study also looked at how the public accounting firms were addressing issues of work and personal life balance for all employees.

The AICPA study indicated that while hiring of females for professional staff positions was slightly more than 50 percent of all new hires, there did appear to be some significant "glass ceiling" issues in the industry. On average, only 12 percent of partners were female. In the largest accounting firms, that is, those with more than 200 employees, the percentage of female partners was even worse at only 5 percent. More importantly, it did not appear that these percentages showed any signs of changing soon. A review of the gender distribution of new partners in the larger firms indicated that almost 90 percent were male. An oil light was starting to go on in the industry.

Some other findings related to turnover also caused concern in the industry. The turnover rate for women was higher than for men at the level just below partners. The trend across the industry showed that more women were leaving accounting firms just before they got high enough in the organization to be considered for partnership. Therefore, even if the partners' admission process was equitable, there were fewer women available to be promoted because they would have already left the organization.

The report summarized the key diversity issues that seemed to be particularly relevant for the accounting profession. These were:

- Work-load issues significantly affected work/personal life balance for both males and females in the industry.

- There was an inaccurate but widespread perception in the industry that women leave public accounting after having children. The reality was that almost 90 percent returned to work after childbirth.

- Sexist attitudes towards women among peers and clients had begun increasing sexual tension in the workplace.

- There was a widespread lack of female role models at senior levels in most firms in the industry.

To asses its own effectiveness as an employer, Ernst & Young conducted its own survey. Diversity issues, including those that surfaced through the AICPA study, were included.

Shelley Pearlman, Director of Diversity, describes how the process unfolded after the survey had been conducted. "For Ernst & Young it began with our Employer Effectiveness Survey. We wanted to take the temperature of the firm to find out how the employees felt about working for E&Y. For the most part, the responses we received were very positive but some diversity related issues did come up particularly related to gender, leave of absences, the perception of women in the firm with regard to their eligibility for partnership, and balancing work and family commitments."

As a result of these findings, E&Y put together a national task force focusing on equitable opportunity. The mandate was to figure out what was really going on, what was behind these diversity issues at E&Y. The task force was headed by Colleen McMorrow, a CA herself, and the office managing partner of the firm's Mississauga office. The task force also included men and women from the firm, across Canada. To identify any trends, the task force reviewed quantitative data specifically in the areas of recruiting, promotion, performance appraisals, and retention. The task force also did a preliminary analysis of how diversity issues were affected by specific aspects of the employment system such as performance appraisals, communications, and legislated employment equity programs.

The task force discovered that there were some diversity issues across the firm. For example, after reviewing the quantitative data, the retention of women in the firm reflected the trends identified in the AICPA report.

As a result of the preliminary review, the task force hired an independent consultant to conduct a more complete qualitative analysis of the organization. The objectives of this assessment were to define the specific diversity themes within Ernst & Young. A theme was defined as a commonly held employee perception that was apparent throughout the organization.

The major vehicle used to gather the qualitative information was a series of focus groups. Participants were chosen from various locations, organizational levels, and functions. The intention was to allow the executive of the organization to fully understand the employees' perceptions about the key diversity themes. It was also thought that this information would indicate whether the firm's ability to attract and retain highly competent professionals was in jeopardy.

Interviews were also conducted with members of the executive group. In these interviews it was evident that the executive group and senior management didn't always have the same perceptions as the employees. It was also evident that not all members of the senior group had appreciated the substantial business benefits that could accrue to the firm by addressing diversity issues.

McMorrow remembers, "When the results of the focus groups were presented to the executive team, they were very surprised with some of the findings. A gap between the executive perception of the firm and the employees' reality was clearly evident. Prior to this feedback, senior management believed that E&Y was the employer of choice for the industry and people were treated fairly. They were very shocked to learn that wasn't how the employees saw the situation."

The combination of the original AICPA survey, the Employer Effectiveness Survey, the employee focus groups, and the executive interviews had succeeded in identifying the relevant diversity issues for Ernst & Young. The issues were clustered into several themes such as questioning women's competence and commitment, appropriate role models for success, gender bias in assignments, balancing work and family, and access to informal networks.

Members of the task force recognized these were substantial issues for the business but they now had to get senior management to understand the links.

STEP 3: LINKING RELEVANT DIVERSITY ISSUES WITH E&Y BUSINESS OBJECTIVES

Once the information was gathered from employee surveys and focus groups, the organization had a clear idea of the relevant diversity issues. The next step was to convince the executive and senior management group that these issues could affect their business.

The CEO of the organization, Ron Gage, wanted to close the gap between the employees' perception of diversity at E&Y and the executives' perception. Gage reminded the other executive members that "E&Y spends more on its human capital than on any other resource, thus the diversity issues must not be seen as an extra, to be accomplished after other business objectives. They go hand in hand to help E&Y achieve those objectives."

The task force made a number of recommendations to the executive, and showed the clear link between the diversity issues and E&Y's business objectives. One of the recommendations was for a champion of diversity to be designated. The CEO, Ron Gage, assumed this role. As well, the position of Director of Diversity was created which Shelly Pearlman assumed. Assuming the executive would acknowledge that employees had perceived inequity in the system, then it would be relatively easy to show how this could affect the firm's bottom line.

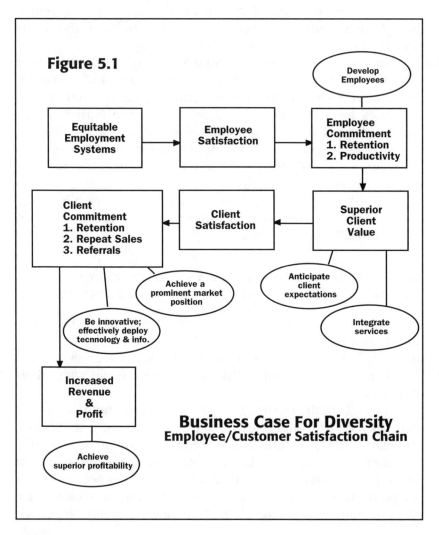

Figure 5.1

Develop Employees

Equitable Employment Systems → Employee Satisfaction → Employee Commitment
1. Retention
2. Productivity

Client Commitment
1. Retention
2. Repeat Sales
3. Referrals ← Client Satisfaction ← Superior Client Value

Achieve a prominent market position

Anticipate client expectations

Be innovative; effectively deploy technology & info.

Integrate services

Increased Revenue & Profit

Business Case For Diversity
Employee/Customer Satisfaction Chain

Achieve superior profitability

Pearlman says, "The successful implementation of diversity must be tied into employee retention. High turnover in a professional services firm is very expensive. Not just the up-front cost of hiring and the transition period but in customer relationships and service. At the end of the day, you have to believe that if you have satisfied employees, they will provide better service to customers. As a result we keep a strong customer base which can result in repeat business and referrals, which in turn builds the business resulting in higher profitability."

To Develop Our People

The most direct link is the E&Y commitment to develop their people. The new human resource direction was to lead to an environment that was attractive to high-quality people in order to retain and fully utilize them.

Executive members were told that the research indicated that inequity present in the E&Y employment system substantially affects employee satisfaction and this appears to be affecting the retention of high-calibre employees. This was especially the case for highly skilled women. If the firm was to meet its stated objective, it had to become more sensitive to the needs of people. Ignoring the employee feedback and the quantitative "oil lights" would run counter to the firm's stated objective and new human resource direction.

Ron Gage says, "Diversity is critically important to maintaining E&Y's position as a leader in the business community. We need the best people to serve our clients. They come from various backgrounds. To build long-term relationships with clients, we need an environment where the best people stay and flourish. And if our people leave to become clients and prospects, we need to ensure their experience allows them to become ambassadors for the firm."

Client Expectations

It was shown how the identified diversity issues could also affect E&Y's ability to anticipate and meet client expectations. The firm was committed to providing high-quality solutions and relevant action-oriented findings on time and at competitive costs.

It became evident that by ignoring the diversity issues, costs would be adversely affected—for example, litigation costs resulting from possible discrimination or harassment charges. It was also pointed out that such charges are inconsistent with clients' expectations of the firm to maintain the highest professional standards of competence, integrity, and objectivity.

Furthermore, many E&Y clients already have a diverse work force. There is every reason to think that if the firm is optimizing all its human resources that it too would start to reflect the diversity of the work force. In fact, there could be missed business opportunities for the firm where the client base includes decision makers from diverse backgrounds while E&Y's audit and consulting teams remain homogeneous.

Teamwork and Integration of Services

The E&Y objective to integrate all available services was also affected by diversity issues. It was argued that unresolved diversity issues could inhibit effective teamwork, especially between males and females. For example, there was some evidence to suggest that women were being denied access to informal networks within E&Y. This was not based on any malicious intent—it was merely the way certain social activities, for example golf, had traditionally been structured. The new focus on teamwork demanded that any barriers that prevented the total integration of all team members be addressed. Ignoring such issues could lead to less-than-ideal decisions and reduced value to the client.

Innovation and Market Positioning

E&Y sought to develop a reputation in the market for thoughtful leadership and innovative solutions. The executive realized that ignoring the identified diversity issues could make the firm appear unresponsive to changing societal values and simply out of touch with the realities of the new work force. For example, work and family issues are a reality for every organization today, given the changing nature of the work force. E&Y could be a leader in showing other employers how to implement alternative work arrangements in a time when balancing work and family is increasingly difficult. The firm could actually create a model for how work should be organized in the next millennium.

Superior Profitability

The most important link between diversity and the E&Y business objectives relates to their quest for superior profitability. The organization intends to achieve this by satisfying their clients, managing costs and productivity effectively, and optimizing all resources. This is the argument made in the business case chart on page 90 and ultimately the major reason that most senior leadership commitment begins to shift as they give more time, energy, and financial resources to the issue and exhibit behavioural modelling for others. Once the leadership understands the benefits of the diversity initiative to the firm's bottom line, they are likely to offer support.

SUMMARY

Ernst & Young, as with many organizations in today's economy, is being required to do more with less. They are required to get more out of their employees, but as Ron Gage notes, the work force has changed, and as a result business has to change. He says, "Business needs to be more flexible in accommodating a diverse work force. All firms need to be open to non-traditional alternatives that satisfy people's needs, otherwise the chain which results in increased profits will break down. E&Y is a customer-driven organization. We are here to serve our clients with excellence. Our employees will not be able to serve our customers with excellence if they are not treated fairly."

What can we learn from the E&Y case? The first lesson is to be clear about what the objectives of the business are. The Ernst & Young vision statement lays out five key areas:

- Building long-term relationships with our clients through service excellence, as the leading, most innovative, integrated professional services firm.

- Meeting the changing expectations of our clients by continuously improving the value of our services.

- Earning the public's trust through our integrity, objectivity, and competence.

• Developing high-performance people as our staff, partners, and alumni.

• Achieving the respect of our clients, the fulfilment of our people, a prominent market position, and a superior level of profitability.

The firm has managed to link the identified issues of diversity with these key business objectives. It has incorporated these objectives in a diversity vision statement. By creating this link, the organization can ensure that the diversity program will survive changes in government, changes in altruistic intentions or pressure from over-zealous advocacy groups. Diversity has been integrated into the way the organization operates.

In Ron Gage's words, "Recognizing the value of a diverse work force is key to maintaining our firm's competitive edge. In fact, we cannot achieve our vision without it, because Mission Millennium is founded on people: clients and ourselves. We need the best people to serve our clients. To build long-term relationships with these clients, we need an environment where the best people stay and flourish."

CIBC: LINKING DIVERSITY TO THE CHANGING MARKETPLACE

In the last chapter, we highlighted the increasing number of organizations that are pursuing diversity to gain access to lucrative "new" markets both domestically and internationally. The Conference Board of Canada has surveyed many of these organizations and reports that almost 70 percent of the senior management team had identified ethno-cultural changes as an important element in overall sales and marketing strategies. Many of these customer-focused organizations actively include diversity in marketing, sales, and customer service strategies.

An example is the Canadian Imperial Bank of Commerce. This organization is federally regulated to pursue a legislated employment equity program. Yet it has gone past the legislative requirements to embrace diversity as one of its key principles.

Al Flood, the chairman and chief executive officer says, "Diversity is not a philosophical discussion. It is part of CIBC right now. The strength and value of our diversity strategy has never been clearer. As we build momentum towards our goal of becoming the pre-eminent Canadian financial services company, we need to capitalize on our diverse work force to help us meet the needs of our diverse customer base. We know that no two employees have the same background, knowledge, and strengths. By taking advantage of our diversity, we can meet and exceed the expectations of our customers."

CIBC has included diversity as part of its strategic plan. As such, the organization has moved past seeing this as a numbers issue and is measuring the progress of its diversity strategy in five ways.

The measurement categories are:

1. Employee perception — How employees feel about CIBC as an employer.

2. Public perception — How the public sees CIBC as an organization.

3. Leadership — Its reputation in the market.

4. Business integration — How diversity is incorporated in day-to-day activities.

5. Work-force representation — The representation of groups at various levels of CIBC.

Judy Jaeger is the director of the Office for Equity and Diversity. She helped design these new measures, which allow the bank to take a more holistic approach to the issue than merely complying with federal employment equity legislation. She says, "Equity and diversity are integral to the bank's ability to meet its business objectives."

An example of this is the bank's focus on business opportunities in the various aboriginal communities. Many aboriginal bands in Canada have received large financial settlements for land claims that have been in dispute for years. Typically, these multi-million-dollar settlements are managed by the leadership of the aboriginal band.

The CIBC and other banks are beginning to recognize the business opportunities that exist in these communities, and many of the banks have appointed vice-presidents of aboriginal business and are ensuring services are sensitive to the various native cultures.

The CIBC is putting a concerted effort into understanding aboriginal communities and their particular needs. It has developed a two-day aboriginal business relationship seminar, which provides an overview of the aboriginal market segment. In the Regina area, where many of the bank's branches are close to major aboriginal communities, staff attend aboriginal awareness workshops. These workshops are intended to allow CIBC customer-service representatives to understand their aboriginal customers' unique financial needs.

One of the seminar leaders, Ron Scrimshaw, believes that a focused approach must be taken to serve native customers. He says, "How well we do is largely dependent on how well our aboriginal customers like dealing with our employees. One solution is to have more aboriginal staff; the other is to train non-native staff." As a result, the bank's Alberta and Northwest Territories business region has set far more aggressive representation goals than the government requires for the number of aboriginal employees it wants to recruit.

CIBC Wood Gundy is the investment arm of the bank and has also endorsed diversity for reasons related to the changing marketplace. Its clients come from all parts of the world. They have complex needs that can't be met with cookie-cutter solutions. So the organization has combined employees with very different backgrounds into teams that attempt to create value-added solutions for clients. These teams reflect their customers and thus have a better chance of understanding what their customers value.

The organization has found that there are spin-off benefits to this approach. Employees have started to learn from one another and are building stronger, more interdependent partnerships. In the words of John Hunkin, the president of CIBC Wood Gundy, "the organization benefits from diversity because our return on expertise is enhanced." The employees benefit through learning opportunities that focus different skills and experiences on common organizational goals.

DIVERSITY: MORE THAN A HUMAN RESOURCES INITIATIVE

The ability to link the diversity strategy to some part of the business strategy is a key component to an effective program. We have seen how in the case of Ernst & Young and the CIBC, the motivation for the program does not require any artificial, external impetuses such as government or political pressure.

There is, however, a common link between the two approaches and that is the endorsement of senior executives. Ron Gage at Ernst & Young, Al Flood at CIBC, and John Hunkin at CIBC Wood Gundy take on responsibility for ensuring the integration of diversity into the workings of the business. Senior executive support is a very critical variable to the successful incorporation of diversity into a business strategy.

In the next chapter, we will see how to get executive and senior management support for the diversity initiative. By achieving this support, the initiative is moved outside the purview of human resources and is integrated into the day-to-day workings of the organization. When the most senior levels of management make diversity one of their public goals, employees recognize it as an important business initiative and are more likely to buy in.

This buy-in can be further deepened if the organization can show a causal link between a diversity strategy and organizational profitability.

ACHIEVING MANAGEMENT COMMITMENT TO AND EMPOYEE AWARENESS OF DIVERSITY

In the last chapter we reviewed the necessity of linking diversity with some element of the business strategy. By creating these links, the organization is assured that the strategy will survive political and legislative changes. A diversity strategy linked to business results will also provide a more powerful motivation for senior leaders in an organization who may have little understanding of diversity issues and even less understanding of how they affect business.

In this chapter we will concentrate on how to bring the diversity messages to senior management and other employees in the organization. We will see how by achieving a strong level of senior commitment the organization can create several key opinion leaders who will bring about substantial corporate change. We will then look at how to communicate these key messages to the remainder of the organization to achieve the desired shift in corporate culture.

The chapter will outline three separate components of achieving executive commitment and employee awareness.

These are:

1. Executive briefing sessions

2. Communications strategies

3. Education strategies

National Grocers/Loblaws is a large retailer headquartered in the southern Ontario area. The organization has moved through each one of these stages to achieve awareness of diversity issues. We will also highlight some of the communication initiatives used by London Life, a leading Canadian insurance company headquartered in southwestern Ontario.

THE EXECUTIVE BRIEFING SESSION

The major purpose of the executive briefing is to get members of the executive to publicly acknowledge that their organization is not a Five. This is not easy.

As we found in the Ernst & Young case study, many times members of the senior executive group do not view the issues of diversity the same way employees do. In many cases, the executive feel that diversity issues are "non-issues"—i.e., their organization already treats people fairly. These executives also assume that employees regard the organization as a good place to work. It is difficult for many executive members to hear that possible inequity exists in their system.

This denial is easy to understand. The executive group is charged with the responsibility of leading the organization. Most executives think they have done a good job of creating a company that treats people fairly regardless of gender, race, creed, etc. These executives are also very loyal to the organization and understandably protective of its reputation. When they begin to listen to negative feedback about the employment system, be it from an external consultant or an internal human resource representative, they may naturally exhibit some resistance.

This is why it is important to first identify a champion for the diversity initiative. The champion is actually a member of the executive team who understands diversity and believes inequity is an issue in the company. The champion need not be the most senior member of the executive such as the CEO or president. He or she merely needs to be a member of the executive who has regular access to their meetings where the business agenda is built. The champion will ensure that the diversity vision stays on the business agenda regardless of competing issues. A good champion will help reduce the resistance to some of the messages surrounding inequity in the organization.

David Williams is the CEO and president of National Grocers Co. Ltd. He is also the avowed champion of the National Grocers diversity program. Williams epitomizes the characteristic of a good champion: he has both heart and head for the issues of diversity. That is, he intellectually understands the business case but is also committed to doing what it takes to reduce inequities in the system. As a good champion, Williams has moved past politically correct communications about diversity issues. To quote one National Grocers employee, "Williams doesn't just talk the talk, he walks the talk. He actually believes this stuff!"

The major responsibility of the champion is to lead a substantial corporate change that will be evolutionary, not revolutionary. Therefore the champion will be required to continually articulate the vision of getting to a Five, especially when resistance occurs. The first duty of the champion is to move the diversity initiative out of the responsibility of human resources and begin to move it on to the executive agenda where it involves all key opinion leaders in the organization. Rob Rochon, Director of Diversity, talks about how this was started with the executive group at National Grocers. "At National Grocers we are very fortunate to have a leader like Dave Williams. He is a true visionary with the ability to put action behind his beliefs. And he believes in the power of diversity. We needed to translate his passion and belief to everyone in our organization. We began by generating a lot of awareness within the senior level of the organization. Our first step was to educate our executives on the changing demographics of our market. We focused heavily on statistics and with that data, looked at the reality of the situation over time. We looked at the changing consumer and found that the source of our market is dramatically changing. Our customer base was significantly affected by new immigrants and their changing consumer needs. Williams used this information to convince the other members of the executive that if we didn't address the needs, wants, desires of our customer base, given the competition we have, we wouldn't be able to survive."

National Grocers still had to make the connection between the raw research and diversity. This was done by organizing a three-hour special briefing session to allow the executive to make the connection between the statistics and their business.

There are certain realities to be considered when this type of executive briefing is being organized. These are:

1. A lack of awareness regarding diversity issues.

2. Hostility caused by legislated fairness fallout.

3. Apathy regarding diversity issues in light of pressing business needs.

Lack of Awareness

One of the most common realities to be considered before conducting an executive briefing is that the executive may have little or no idea about the issues surrounding diversity—many of them have probably had little first-hand exposure to inequity because of the composition of the group.

The majority of senior executives across Canada are from a relatively homogeneous group, which is usually white, able-bodied, upper-middle-class, heterosexual, sole-earner, Christian males. A 1992 study of Canadian executives by *Canadian Business* magazine found that less than .04 percent of executives did not fit this picture. It is unlikely that members of this group have faced discrimination related to their gender, race, culture, language, nationality, or sexual orientation. Thus it may be difficult for them to empathize with issues such as sexism, racism, homophobia, or even systemic inequities such as inflexible maternity policies. This does not mean that these people are out of touch—it is just that their life reality is probably dissimilar to the average employee.

For example, we have seen that the majority of the work force today comes from dual-earner households. This reality substantially affects work and family balance issues. Most executives come from the traditional sole-earner model, in which the husband goes to work and the wife stays home to handle domestic responsibilities, including child care. It may be hard for many executives to imagine the challenges faced by dual-earner or single parents because they have never faced these circumstances themselves.

People have a tough time recognizing discrimination if they themselves have never experienced it. It may be difficult for men to recognize sexism or for heterosexuals to see the realities of homophobia. This is just human nature. Senior executives are no different. If they have not faced inequitable treatment based on their group status, they may take a "say it ain't so" attitude in the executive briefing. A presenter should expect this as a normal reaction.

The National Grocers executive briefing was no different although the organization is known in the industry for its progressive people policies. Many of the executive members firmly believed the company lived its human resource vision statement, that "people are the driving force to excellence." Yet even here we ran into senior executives who could not relate to the diversity issues being relevant for their organization.

I remember having an off-line conversation with one executive in the briefing session who was deeply disturbed that we could be inferring that sexism existed in his work force. He was convinced that his company treated women as well as men and was unwilling to consider possible sexism. I asked him if his wife worked outside the home. It turned out she did not but his daughter did. In fact, his daughter worked for the company. I asked him to have a conversation with her that night about the amount of sexism she has faced in the workplace and then call me the next day. The next day he called me and told me the conversation with his daughter had lasted three hours and was deeply disturbing for him. He had not realized the extent of sexism she had faced in the workplace. But he did admit that after a couple of hours of listening to her, he began to realize that she had told him about many of these things before but he had never really listened to her.

The executive briefing can be a good place to acknowledge the existence of diversity but the presenter must be prepared to deal with a low level of awareness among the executive. The presenter needs to be able to empathize with the perspective of executive members and then use objective information to allow them to understand the issues.

Hostile Reactions

A more difficult situation than ignorance is dealing with the hostility towards diversity that may have been caused by legislated fairness programs. Here again, the composition of the audience is a relevant factor. Remember that the one group legislated fairness programs usually left out was white able-bodied males— the very group likely to be represented on the executive committee. It is highly likely that some members of the executive will resist a diversity program because they resent the messages inherent in the legislated fairness debate.

Earlier, we looked at the tendency of legislated fairness programs to blame one group for the discrimination being faced by the so-called designated groups. The group blamed was white able-bodied males. A curious paradox of the legislated fairness phenomenon was that this was probably the most important group that had to buy in to the legislative requirements if they were to be viable. That is to say, if the senior executives of major companies refused to comply, then the effectiveness of the legislation would be severely limited.

The guilt-ridden approach taken by advocates of legislative fairness has caused many executives to react with "white male backlash." An article entitled "Backlash—The Challenge to Diversity Training" recently appeared in *Training & Development* magazine. It warned trainers of the realities of this type of reaction. It says, "Young and old, men are reacting against the Demonic White European Male syndrome, the perceived opinion that white males are responsible for every ill." The article goes on to caution trainers about assuming that the point of diversity training is to change these "demonic" white males.

Beating up on white males reinforces an "us versus them" approach to issues of diversity and breeds resentment, fear, and eventually backlash. This is clearly the reality in many executive briefings. The presentation actually becomes a lecture on the privileges of having white skin in a male body. One equity manager recounted an executive briefing with a consultant who specializes in the "white-male guilt" approach. She explained how her executive was asked to write down all the powers they had in their workplace because of their white race. Then the participants were forced to admit how the "currency of being white" contributed to systemic racism. Needless to say, the presentation turned into a highly emotional, angry battle between the consultant and the executive. The presentation was cut short and the diversity initiative was delayed several months.

The way to overcome the resistance of white male backlash is to take the inclusive approach to the issue of diversity and link it to the bottom line. At National Grocers, Rob Rochon accomplished this by moving out of the "us versus them" approach to the inclusive approach of understanding all differences in light of the changing demographics of the workplace and market. He says "We asked ourselves, 'Do we really welcome people into our company who are different? Do we support a culture that is accommodating to all groups?'"

To answer those questions, the organization began to clarify what the changing demographics meant to their market base. The senior executive came away with the belief that regardless of the differences between people, they had a business responsibility to serve all consumers and meet their needs.

Apathy

Executives in today's organizations face daunting business agendas. The items range from issues of changing government regulations to increased competition to reducing costs to improving productivity and so forth. One of the major challenges of the executive briefing is to ignite interest in this apparent soft issue in the face of these substantial business concerns. Executive apathy towards diversity is perhaps one of the most difficult conditions to overcome. Rob Rochon explains: "The demographic research we presented was all well received but at the end of each presentation, the most frequently asked question was 'so what?' The statistics told a story and we applied it to our marketplace, but for some executives it was tough to make the connection between the statistics and our profitability."

Most senior executives spend their time focusing on profit

goals and market share. If they are presented with issues that do not directly affect either of these, there is good reason to expect them to see the issues as irrelevant. If the issues are considered irrelevant, they will likely be ignored. This is frequently the case for diversity issues. Executives do not make the connection between these so-called "soft" people issues and their bottom line. The challenge of the executive briefing is to make this link.

The way to do this is to show how the people issues actually drive profitability within the organization. In an earlier chapter, we introduced the model for the business case for equity. This model attempts to link employee satisfaction, loyalty, and productivity to the value of products and services delivered so that an organization can build customer satisfaction and loyalty that will increase profitability and growth. In order to overcome executive apathy, the links in this model must be proven. The executive must be shown how an increase in the equitable treatment of employees positively influences the bottom line.

In order to prove the links in the model, an organization must have measurement techniques that can put a "hard value" on "soft measures." For example, if an organization can prove that if it reduces workplace harassment by 20 percent, it will improve worker satisfaction by 50 percent, which translates through the model to improved customer satisfaction of 75 percent, then it has begun to make the links between issues of diversity and the traditional business issues. It is a short jump from improved customer satisfaction to issues of market share and profit. For example, a *Harvard Business Review* article published in October 1990, entitled, "Zero Defections: Quality Comes to Services," authors Reichheld and Sasser estimated that a 5 percent increase in customer satisfaction can substantially improve customer loyalty, producing profit increases from 25 percent to 85 percent.

Measuring customer satisfaction and employee opinions has become a regular part of doing business today. But rarely is a correlation made between the two measures. Employee satisfaction surveys have become routine annual occurrences but the information gathered is rarely used effectively. An organization must ensure that employee satisfaction is being measured in a way to link it to similar measures of customer satisfaction. Once this link has been developed, the organization can establish overall trends and determine how improving the environment for employees affects their bottom line. For example, Taco Bell studies employee satisfaction using several techniques such as surveys, focus groups, interviews, and roundtable meetings. Customer satisfaction is measured by conducting biannual interviews with customers that include similar questions about satisfaction with employee friendliness and effort. The employee and customer satisfaction rankings for each store are correlated so that the company can see the overall trends and links between employee and customer satisfaction.

In an upcoming chapter we will introduce the qualitative variables that must be measured in employee satisfaction to begin making these links.

SUMMARY

The executive briefing is a key element in achieving senior commitment to the diversity program. Its primary purpose is to have the leaders of the organization publicly admit that they may have been "living a lie" on the merit principle. That is, their employment system, like any other, contains certain inequities that inhibit the hiring, promotion, and retention of the most productive employees. This initial acknowledgement is essential in order to get "buy in" from some of the most important key opinion leaders in the organization.

In order for the executive briefing to be successful, various responses should be anticipated. The executive may be either unaware of, hostile towards, or apathetic about the diversity issues. Thus the presentation must include the endorsement of a strong champion and use a convincing, fact-based business argument. Once the executive is onside, the program turns to communicating and educating the remainder of the work force.

THE COMMUNICATIONS STRATEGY

The design of an effective communications strategy is one of the most important preparatory exercises to be completed in a diversity strategy. As with the executive briefing, it is important to acknowledge that the environment for the introduction of the diversity strategy may be poisoned due to perceptions caused by legislated fairness. Ignoring this poisoned environment could sabotage a well-thought-out diversity program even before it begins.

Many organizations complying with legislated fairness requirements choose a minimalist approach to communicating issues associated with diversity. The logic is to attempt to avoid dealing with some of the more contentious issues of the legislated equity debate such as quotas, reverse discrimination, and tokenism. The leaders of this type of organization may feel that, given the existing environment surrounding equity issues, the less information conveyed to employees the better.

An organization approaching diversity from a business perspective will take the opposite approach. It will seek to maximize the effectiveness of a diversity strategy by pursuing a full-fledged, proactive, communications strategy. Its logic is that the diversity initiative is good news for the employees, a positive signal that the organization seeks to create fairer employment systems for everyone.

London Life Insurance Group is a well-known Canadian insurance company and one of the largest employers in the London, Ontario, area. On February 2, 1995, the front-page story of its internal newspaper, *Focus*, announced an "upbeat, positive, exhilarating" video that was to be distributed and shown in all London Life offices to "allow everyone in the company to learn about diversity and the strategic role it plays." The article outlined the business case for equity in light of changing demographics in the marketplace and workplace. It included quotations from the president and the senior vice-president, who had volunteered to be the champions for the initiative.

In the video, the President of the organization, Gord Cunningham, explains, "We're committed to absolute fairness in our employment practices. We know that this contributes to increased productivity and job satisfaction. Today we are reviewing our policies, practices, and procedures relating to recruiting, hiring, promotion, and training to ensure that we are being fair to everyone. Our ability to continue to play an important role in shaping the life and health industry in Canada will, in great part, depend on being able to attract and retain the best possible people."

Unlike the exclusionary, blame-tainted messages in the legislative approach, this is a good-news message for every employee. It is inclusive, business-oriented, and meant to create a win for employees and the company. The message is simple, understandable, and one that the organization can be proud to articulate. And it will.

The interesting thing is that the London Life approach will avoid all the usual contentious issues that are evoked by legislation because it has chosen to communicate the issue from a business perspective. Crafting a strong communications strategy with a beginning (i.e., a launch), a middle, and an end will allow employees to understand the logic behind some of the activities in the diversity strategy. This understanding will lead to more active participation by employees, which will prevent having to repeat key activities such as the quantitative and qualitative survey.

It is likely that the design of an effective communications strategy will require the expertise of a communications expert. Issues surrounding discrimination and harassment have rarely been raised publicly in the work force. Knowing how to effectively communicate these types of contentious issues requires specialized skill. It is important that the human resource professional seek out this expertise to help design the communications strategy.

It is also important to assess the current communications process within the organization before an effective strategy is designed. This assessment should include a review of how the organization currently communicates, who the primary audiences for communication are, what vehicles are used to communicate to these audiences, and the result of previous communication attempts. This assessment of the current communications process and an objective review of its effectiveness should be the first step in the development of a diversity communications plan.

Let us now look at the key components of an effective diversity communications plan.

Developing an Effective Diversity Communications Plan

Any good communications plan must address the following questions:

1. Why do you want to communicate?

2. What do you want to communicate?

3. How do you want to communicate?

4. What results do you want to achieve?

Let's examine the answers to these four questions in detail.

1. Why Do You Want to Communicate?

Organizations will communicate their position on diversity to leverage their competitive positioning and to enhance support for their strategic vision and mission. Rob Rochon of National Grocers explains how they attempted to do this: "We found we had to go right back and understand our business issues, the change in the consumer, and how both of these elements affected the competition for grocery dollars in the local communities where we have our stores. Our senior executives held a series of meetings where they formulated core values and operating principles and connected them to valuing diversity and equitable employment systems.

"We then positioned ourselves with our employees and informed them why we were going down the diversity path. This allowed our employees to know why valuing diversity is important and how it connects to our profitability as a business."

It will be important at this stage in the process to identify the key audiences for the communications program. Audiences will be from the following groups:

- Customers

- Influencers (both internal and external)

- Communities

- Investors, financial community

- Employees
- Trade associations
- Sales force, distribution network
- Other key stakeholders

Each audience should be analyzed to identify (based on your assessment of past communications to your particular audiences) which will be targets for diversity messages. Objectives should then be set for each target audience, that is, do you want to inform, persuade, or motivate each particular audience? Once you have identified the audiences for your communications, you should decide what it is you wish to communicate to each audience.

2. What Do You Want to Communicate?

It is especially important to acknowledge the level of misinformation and misunderstanding surrounding issues of diversity and equity. Communications around these issues will be particularly challenging because of the contentious nature of the subject matter and the levels of hostility and backlash that could be part of the diversity landscape.

In formulating key messages, it will be crucial to address areas of contention head-on and to ensure that your organization's positioning on these issues is clear. Here are some suggestions about the messages that should be included in any diversity communications plan.

A good communication strategy begins with crafting a clear policy statement regarding diversity. In an organization approaching the issue from a business perspective, this statement will be inclusive of all employees. Dow Chemical Canada Inc. has crafted such a statement that has been communicated directly to every Dow employee. It reads: "One of the most important characteristics of the Dow Chemical Company is our diversity—diversity in our products, our market, and our people. Dow's diversity of employees positively influences our ideas and work styles. We are different from each other in many ways (education, age, gender, style, ethnicity, culture). We believe these individual differences, combined with talent and vision, enrich us as a company and help ensure our future success.

"By creating a work environment that recognizes, values and manages diversity in our work force, we will have initiated a cultural change within Dow. Success in diversity will enhance the success of Dow people, shareholders, customers, and society."

There are a couple of important things to note about the Dow diversity statement. The first thing is that it is inclusive. It goes past race and gender, the more typical issues associated with diversity. This allows all employees to see the relevance of the diversity program to their personal situation. Secondly, the statement clearly articulates that this is being pursued to enhance the effectiveness of the business, not to comply with legislation or to be politically correct. This type of statement can serve as the cornerstone of an effective communications strategy.

Key Message 1: What Is Diversity?

Diversity is the recognition and acknowledgement of individual differences. In a diverse work force, such as we have today, treating people equally may mean ignoring individual differences. This can lead to inequitable treatment. An organization practising diversity seeks to provide equitable treatment for all employees. The organization does this by moving past equal treatment, where differences are ignored, to equitable treatment, where differences are recognized, acknowledged, and eventually valued.

Key Message 2: The Business Approach

The most important message to be communicated is that the organization is pursuing diversity for business reasons. As we have said earlier, these reasons could be related to either the changing marketplace or workplace. Once employees understand the business rationale behind the program, cynical attitudes about legislated compliance will be reduced.

Rochon explains how National Grocers attempted to communicate the business approach in a legislated environment. "The change in government occurred at about the same time we came to the realization that diversity and improving market share went hand in hand. We believed at the time that the new NDP government was going to bring in oppressive employment equity legislation. We saw an opportunity to get ahead of the government by communicating that we were pursuing ethical employment standards for business reasons."

Communicating the business argument for diversity in a legislated environment is admittedly more difficult because employees are bound to feel the organization is pursuing the initiative because it has to. Nevertheless, the communications strategy must clearly articulate the links between the equity issues and the business.

Key Message 3: The Goal of the Diversity Strategy — Equitable Employment Systems

It is important that employees understand that the diversity strategy is meant to create an equitable employment system. We have defined an equitable employment system as a system based on fairness and merit that allows an organization to attract and retain the most qualified work force regardless of sex, race, ethnicity, class, disability, sexual orientation, or any other non-job-related criteria. A proper communications strategy must clearly articulate this as the goal of any diversity program.

The communications strategy should also distinguish between an equitable employment system and legislated employment equity. The major distinction is that the former is about creating fair employment systems for all employees. The latter concerns the creation of fair systems for government-designated disadvantaged groups. Thus a legislated employment equity program is about fairness for some. A diversity program is always about equity for all.

Key Message 4: The Key Elements of the Diversity Plan

An organization should communicate those areas of the diversity plan that will require employee participation. These areas are:

• The employment systems review

• The quantitative and qualitative surveys

• The mandate and membership of the diversity advisory committee

• The consultation process with employees

These elements will be described in more detail in upcoming chapters, but the communications strategy should include them as an important message.

Once you have agreed on the key messages you need to deliver, it will be important to decide on the communications vehicles that will deliver those messages.

3. How Do You Want to Communicate?

There are a number of communication vehicles that are effective in delivering your key equity and diversity messages. It is important to go back and review the vehicles that you are currently using and assess their effectiveness. If you have determined that some of your current vehicles are not achieving the results you would like, you now have the opportunity to find new ways to reach existing audiences.

Possible vehicles for communication of the diversity message are:

- Memos

- Newsletters

- Videos

- Meetings

- Speeches

- Training programs

- Employee team meetings

- Management team meetings

- Informal networks using key opinion leaders

It will be important to select a vehicle that maximizes audience reach while getting your messages out in a timely manner. We would caution against making the communication of diversity an "event," perceived as short-term, and one that will be another soon-to-be-forgotten "flavour of the week." Merging the diversity message with key themes in the organization will integrate the program into day-to-day workings. Continued communication and reformulating your messages over time will also help to ensure that diversity issues are an integral part of the way your organization conducts business.

It will be important to ensure consistency of messages no matter what vehicle is used. Resources should be assigned to review all communications and review key messages prior to any execution of diversity-related issues. If your organization has a communications specialist, that individual, in conjunction with human resources, would be the ideal reviewer.

While newsletters, speeches by key opinion leaders, and regular communications from senior executives are important parts of any effective communications strategy, we have found that properly designed diversity educational programs are the best way to communicate these issues. Later in the chapter, we will review how to integrate the key diversity messages in an educational program.

Most employees are cynical about communications regarding any business issue. Most of us have heard (all too often) that a particular initiative is essential to the future success of the business. Most organizations have not lived up to the promises they have made in the past with respect to how they have followed through with employees. This is why selecting the right messengers for your diversity communications program is so important.

Top-down as well as bottom-up messengers provide the most positive role models for communication on these issues. Top-down because all employees know that nothing happens in an organization without senior management support. Bottom-up messengers reinforce the idea of employee participation in an ongoing process that is inclusive.

In an upcoming chapter, we will review how to use the diversity advisory committee to aid in communication of diversity initiatives. This group usually represents a cross-section of the organization and can act as internal messengers to consistently reinforce key messages. These committee representatives will also be a valuable source of feedback regarding the effectiveness of diversity messages being communicated throughout the organization.

Once you have determined the appropriate vehicles, it will be important to delineate specifically what it is you want your communications strategy to achieve.

4. What Result Do You Want to Achieve?

It is important to acknowledge the measures of success for a communications program. In a communications program, there are three possible results: to inform, to persuade, and to motivate. Your diversity communications program should seek to achieve the following objectives:

- Inform all audiences of what diversity and equitable employment systems are.

- Obtain a commitment to the diversity strategy and the vision of "equity for all."

- Motivate the debunking of diversity-related myths such as reverse discrimination and tokenism.

- Inform various audiences of the diversity champion and key opinion leaders such as the members of the advisory team.

- Obtain participation in key elements of the diversity program such as the ESR and the surveys.

- Motivate employees to help create discrimination and harassment-free environments.

A proper communications strategy will evolve over time. As you make adjustments to the diversity program, the communications strategy should also be adjusted. Ongoing review of communications objectives and results should ensure that the programs stay consistent with the primary diversity initiatives. It is also important to understand that the level of sophistication of the audience will shift over time and that new messages will need to be developed to ensure that you continue to motivate support and participation for the program.

The Most Commonly Asked Questions

Q) Why are we dwelling on differences? Should we not all strive to be the same?

A)   Every individual is different and can contribute to our organization in different ways. We value these differences because we think they can lead to a more effective organization. Our goal is to acknowledge and transcend these differences to ensure that every individual can make his/her maximum contribution.

Q) Don't present unemployment rates indicate that we will have an increased labour supply in the future?

A)   The present high unemployment rates hide the "skills gap" that exists in Canada. There are many industries that are having difficulty finding skilled individuals for certain occupations. Many of those presently unemployed would require significant retraining to fill these positions.

Q) Will white, able-bodied males be a minority in Canada?

A)   White, able-bodied males will represent approximately 20 percent of net, new entrants to the Canadian work force over the next decade; historically they formed 80 percent. Even at current trends, it will be a long time before white able-bodied males become a minority.

Q) Why do most of our immigrants come from the Third World?

A)   Canada changed its immigration policy in the mid-seventies, which opened the doors to immigrants from countries other than Europe and Britain. As the economies of Europe and Britain have improved, fewer people with the economic characteristics needed in Canada are applying. At the same time, educated and skilled people from the Third World find Canada an attractive alternative.

Q) Are persons with disabilities capable of working full time?

A)   Yes, the substantial improvements in communication and transportation technology have made it possible for many people with disabilities to leave institutions, enter the work force, and work full time.

Q) Do Aboriginal people really want to work and are they qualified?

A)   The unemployment rate for Aboriginal people is significantly higher than the non-Aboriginal community but that should not indicate any lack of desire to work. It is probably related to geography and the lack of economic opportunity caused by the location of reserves. While opportunities for the younger generation are improving, there is still some disparity in the levels of education.

Q) Do we all have stereotypes and prejudices?

A)   All human beings stereotype information in order to help them cat-
egorize things. There is, however, a difference between a stereotype,
and a prejudice, which is a negative attitude or opinion. It is possible to
have a stereotype, which is more neutral, without a prejudice, but it is
unlikely that a person can have a prejudice without a stereotype.

**Q) Shouldn't immigrants be required to conform to
Canadian standards?**

A)   All immigrants go through some level of assimilation to the "Canadian way" but the official policy of multiculturalism encourages a sharing of cultural differences rather than total conformity to one way of life.

**Q) Doesn't accommodation cost more money than it's
worth?**

A)   There are many types of accommodation that have little or no cost;
for example, adjustable computer screens or the recognition of non-
Christian holidays. The benefit of any accommodation must always be
considered along with the cost.

Q) Can you really define sexual harassment?

A)   Yes, there is a legal definition for workplace harassment. It is "a
course of vexatious comment or conduct that is known, or ought reasonably to be known, to be unwelcome."

**Q) Shouldn't men and women be treated the same in the
workplace?**

A)   Men and women are not the same, there are obvious differences
between the sexes. However, both men and women deserve fair treatment in the workplace and this is the goal of diversity.

**Q) What is the difference between the police and fire depart-
ment programs and a diversity program?**

A)   Most police and fire department programs are forms of legislated
fairness like affirmative action. In affirmative action, some agent from outside the organization or work unit sets quotas with respect to the number of designated group members to be hired or promoted. Diversity
foresees the removal of any barriers that may be having an adverse
effect on any group, the development of overall goals and timetables by
the people in the organization, and the hiring and promotion of the best
person for the job regardless of non-job-related criteria.

**Q) What is the difference between pay equity and equitable
employment systems?**

A)   Pay equity was designed to ensure that women received equal pay for work of equal value when compared with men. Equitable employment systems are systems that are fair for all, operate on merit, and are free of any systematic barriers that might have an adverse effect on the hiring or promotion of any group of people.

Q) What is the difference between harassment and discrimination?

A)   Discrimination is defined as the denial of equal treatment, civil liberties, and opportunity to individuals or groups with respect to education, accommodation, health care, employment, and access to services, goods, and facilities. It consists of making unjust distinctions on the basis of race, colour, nationality, sex, age, religion, political affiliation, marital or family status, sexual orientation, and physical, developmental, or mental disability. The roots of discrimination lie in stereotyping and prejudices. Harassment is defined as a course of vexatious comment or conduct that is known or ought reasonably to be known to be unwelcome. Harassment most commonly occurs based on sex, race, or ethnic origin. The roots of harassment lie more in power than in passion. Both discrimination and harassment are prohibited by legislation in all Canadian jurisdictions.

Q) Where does sexual orientation fit with respect to discrimination/harassment?

A)   Sexual orientation usually refers to the rights of people who are openly gay or lesbian. Sexual orientation is a prohibited ground of discrimination in Ontario. It is not presently a prohibited ground of harassment, but this is expected to be changed shortly.

Q) Explain seniority and unions.

A)   Employment systems based on seniority are a basic plank of any collective agreement between a company and a union. It is an almost unassailable principle of unions and is considered to have been won at considerable cost by earlier generations or workers. Senority's predecessors for making decisions regarding promotions, training opportunities, choice of working hours, etc., were favouritism, nepotism, and the like. The basis of seniority is that the person with the longest service gets the first chance. In reverse, when work forces need to be reduced in size, the person with the least seniority goes first. In non-union situations, the equivalent to seniority is service-based entitlements. In the academic world, tenure is a similar concept.

Q) *What is the difference between the American "melting pot" and the Canadian "mosaic" or multiculturalism?*

A)   The prevailing belief in Canada is that Americans "force" immigrants to assimilate to the dominant culture. The equally prevailing belief is that Canadians are more tolerant of minority cultures as reflected in the socio-political policy of multiculturalism. Recent research conducted in Canada by the C.D. Howe Institute and the Canadian Council of Christians and Jews, and in the United States by the National Conference, indicates that the difference between the mosaic and the melting pot is more a myth than it is a reality. While there are differences in emphasis and rhetoric on the subject, the research indicates that on actual cultural retention there are no systematic differences—assimilation rates and economic opportunities for minorities in the two countries are similar. The C.D. Howe Institute study concludes: "The general cultural differences between Canada and the United States imply differences of tone in ethnic and race relations in the two countries. The Canadian style is more low key than the American; moreover, Canadians have a conscious tradition of "tolerance" that Americans do not have. In terms of their effects on the experience of minority groups, however, these differences are more apparent than real."

Q) *What is the difference between diversity and legislated employment equity?*

A)   A diversity program is designed to create an equitable or fair employment system for all employees. The progress of the program is measured by the perception of equity by all employees. The ultimate goal of a diversity program is the achievement of an equitable employment system.

Legislated employment equity is a program designed to correct a past injustice for specified designated groups.

The progress of the program is measured by the numerical representation of these designated groups in a particular work force. The ultimate goal of a legislated employment equity program is government compliance.

Q) *What is the difference between legislated employment equity and affirmative action?*

A)   There are more similarities than differences. Both programs are based on a government attempting to legislate fairness for certain groups. Fairness cannot be legislated. Both programs rely on numerical representation to measure progress. The major difference between employment equity and affirmative action is who sets the number. Affirmative action frequently relies on quotas. A quota is an externally set number by a governement that must be achieved or the employer will face punitive consequences. Employment equity relies on goals and timetables of internally set numbers that are more flexible than quotas. There are usually no punitive consequences for missing a goal.

Q) Why does employment equity and affirmative action legislation only cover certain groups?

A)   The legislators' view is that only certain groups have been disadvantaged in employment. The law is designed to redress the past imbalance and ensure these groups now obtain fair treatment. Other groups are not included apparently because the legislators do not believe any other groups require support to achieve fair treatment.

Q) Will diversity lead to reverse discrimination and tokenism?

A)   A diversity program is designed to create an equitable employment system. An equitable employment system is fair to all groups. It is not possible to be fair to some. Diveristy seeks to create employment systems that are based solely on merit regardless of gender, race, culture, nationality, class, religion, or any other non-job-related criteria. As such, diversity will work against reverse discrimination and tokenism.

Q) Isn't diversity merely about political correctness?

A)   Diversity is about business. It is driven by the changing nature of the Canadian work force and marketplace. These substantial demographic changes will affect every employer across this country in a very real way.

Q) If diversity isn't the same as legislated fairness, why do we collect representation numbers?

A)   In a proper diversity program representation numbers are a signal of inequity in an employment system. The numbers are a means to an end, a signal that something may have gone wrong in the system. The real measure of equity in a proper diversity program will be the measurement of employee opinions that can be used to understand the representation numbers.

Q) Why is diversity an issue today?

A)   In the past, i.e., up until the late 1970s, the North American work force was relatively homogeneous. Eighty percent of net, new entrants were white, able-bodied males. Today, the work force is far more diverse with 80 percent of the work force coming from other groups.

Diversity is an issue today because a diverse work force operates very differently than a homogeneous work force.

Q) What are the major management issues that occur in a diverse work force?

A) Managers were taught to treat all of their employees the same and ignore differences. In a diverse work force equal treatment by managers can lead to inequity. Managers need to learn how to treat employees equitably but not the same. A managing diversity program can lead to these skills.

Q) Why are white males included in a diversity program? Haven't they always received an advantage in employment?

A) Inequity has existed in employment systems against all groups including white males. An equitable employment system is meant to remove discrimination and introduce the merit principle for all.

Q) Will diversity reduce the effort now devoted to gender equity in the workplace?

A) A proper diversity program should include the inequities of all groups but not at the expense of others. Gender equity will be a major part of this initiative.

Q) Is diversity about changing attitudes or changing behaviours?

A) It is obviously easier to change behaviours than attitudes, but a diversity program is about both. It is likely that a change in behaviours such as reducing harassment can be achieved almost immediately through a diversity program. A change in attitude is a more evolutionary process that will come about as people from diverse backgrounds gain experience working with each other.

As mentioned on page 116, an effective educational program can be one of the most valuable communication tools within the organization. Let us now look at how education can be used to create the appropriate environment for the introduction of a successful diversity program.

EDUCATION

A properly designed diversity educational program can accomplish several objectives for the diversity strategy. The major benefits of diversity education are:

- To shift the focus of equity issues from the legislative and social perspective to the business perspective

- To provide answers to the typical "backlash" issues such as reverse discrimination and tokenism

- To educate participants on the highly contentious issues that become more evident in a diverse work force, e.g., sexism, racism, and workplace harassment

- To identify specific attitudinal and systemic inequities in the work force

- To introduce participants to the benefits of a diverse population from a marketing perspective

There is one other key purpose of a properly designed educational program and that is to use it as a vehicle to collect the quantitative and qualitative data necessary for the diversity program.

Let us look at each objective.

Shift the Focus

We have already mentioned that frequently there is a "poisoned environment" surrounding issues of diversity. The term "poisoned environment" is used in the legal profession and usually applies to a work environment that is hostile towards a certain group. When we say there is a poisoned environment surrounding diversity issues we are talking about the hostility that exists about these issues, even before a program has begun. Much of this hostility is generated by the popular misconception that these issues are either about legislation or altruism. This is the case especially when diversity issues are covered by the popular press.

Reporters in the media have the unenviable task of being instant experts on any story they cover. This requires reporters to sometimes take shortcuts that do not allow the reader to put a story into a wider context. At the same time, the reporter must make the story interesting enough to encourage the general public to buy their paper or watch the program. Sensationalism in news stories frequently results. This has clearly happened with the issues that surround equity and diversity.

One of the biggest media stories of the decade was the Hill-Thomas harassment case, which was described by one media analyst as "the most theatrical scandal in Washington history, outdoing the Army-McCarthy, Watergate, and Iran-Contra—a mix of race, ambition, passion, sex, political ideology, and most of all, power." Needless to say, the facts in this case were less important than the story. This is frequently the case when diversity issues are covered in the media. Most diversity issues concerning discrimination and harassment make good stories, in which one side is pitted against the other.

Even less sensational stories than Hill-Thomas have provided the media with plenty of compelling headlines such as "White Males Need Not Apply," "Equity Quotas Scare Firms," "$7.2 Million Harassment Settlement," "Minority Groups Gaining Power" appearing in the popular, mainstream press. In an industry where a good "bad" story frequently sells more papers than a good news story, these headlines are attractive "hooks." Unfortunately, these stories do little to educate people about the real issues.

Every time a story like Hill-Thomas appears in the media, the environment for an effective diversity program can become more poisoned. This negative environment needs to be neutralized by an effective education program before a diversity program is introduced. If not, the program can face significant resistance and can be sabotaged before it begins.

A proper diversity educational program should define three terms that usually do not get distinguished in the popular media. These terms are affirmative action, legislated employment equity, and diversity—the business case for equity. Let us look at how a diversity educational program can provide participants with an understanding of each term.

In Chapter 3 we traced the evolution of legislated fairness programs in North America. We saw that affirmative action programs started in the United States in the sixties as a response to civil rights unrest. In the mid-eighties, Canada began its relationship with legislated fairness, coining a new phrase called employment equity.

Affirmative action and legislated employment equity are similar in many ways. Both programs designate groups for preferential treatment. Both programs are meant to correct past injustices. And both programs rely on numerical representation as the primary measurement of success. Perhaps the major difference between affirmative action and employment equity is the focus on quotas. Quotas are far more common in the U.S. history with legislated fairness than can be seen in Canada. In fact, there is only one recorded case of government-imposed quotas in Canada. This was the case of Canadian National Railways, which was ordered to hire a specific percentage of females for non-traditional jobs in the mid-eighties.

Much criticism of legislated employment equity comes from the confusion between the terms "quotas" and "goals." In fact, it was this confusion that led to the repealing of the employment equity law in Ontario. An educational session can be used to clarify that a quota is an externally set number by government and if missed, the company faces some financial or punitive consequence. A goal is an internally set number used to guide a program and if missed by the company, there is no external consequence. Canadian employment equity legislation has never included quotas, which is the major difference between it and U.S. affirmative action.

An educational program needs to show how diversity moves past the legislative and social realm. Diversity is the business case for equity. Diversity is not pursued because a government is forcing an organization to follow a particular law. It is being pursued because the changing demographics of the work force and the marketplace require a substantial shift in the way the business is operated. Ensuring that employees understand the business motivation for the diversity program can reduce the hostility surrounding equity issues.

National Grocers has improved the environment surrounding diversity issues, by pursuing an aggressive educational program using their own staff. The program links diversity issues to the changing nature of the marketplace. Rob Rochon talks about how the NG diversity educational program is designed: "Dave Williams' mission is to share diversity learning with all employees throughout the National Grocers organization. It was critical to ensure that senior-level management received the learning first so that they could demonstrate their skills through day-to-day actions. They also took responsibility in cascading the learning down throughout the organization. In order to facilitate the cascading process, we began to conduct diversity sessions internally using a 'train the trainer' approach facilitated by an external consultant.

"First, we developed a detailed leader's guide and a video that focused on the whys and whats of diversity. The video combined with the leader's guide resulted in a one-day diversity educational session. Second, we asked our senior board members to recommend an individual from each division to become a facilitator for diversity programs. Third, we job-posted the opportunity. We asked people within the organization if they had an interest in facilitating diversity sessions. We received about 25 volunteers. A selection committee whittled down the list of applicants to six and, combined with the senior board recommendations, we ended up with a facilitator team of fifteen. There were many benefits derived from building the team in this manner—most importantly, the strong cross-functional flavour of the team. For example, there is a store manager, a vice-president of finance, a part-time grocery clerk, and an information service programmer, to name a few.

"Through our educational sessions, we are understanding our business issues better and strengthening the business case for diversity. Our people are beginning to see how valuing diversity can translate into better business results. For example, Dave Williams often says it does not make sense to hire an outside consultant to tell us how to merchandise our stores to an ethnic market when we could just talk to our employees who come from these diverse communities. In an educational session, we can talk to the employees who work in our stores and are face to face with the customers on a day-to-day basis."

The National Grocer's educational program is one of several models that can be used to shift the perspective on diversity issues. Organizations such as IBM have used external resources to present full-day workshops to all their staff while other organizations have used high-technology CD-ROM or video training. Whichever medium is used, shifting to a business perspective is an important objective of the educational component.

Dealing With Backlash Issues

Earlier we spoke about one of the biggest challenges facing diversity practitioners: how to handle backlash issues. The two most common issues are reverse discrimination and tokenism. Reverse discrimination is the perception that everyone but white able-bodied males will benefit from the diversity program. Tokenism is the perception that less qualified members of designated groups will be hired and promoted over more qualified white males.

Most of the perceptions surrounding reverse discrimination come from reactions to legislated fairness programs. Both in the United States and Canada, white able-bodied males were not covered by legislated programs. One equity-seeking advocate explained to me, "White males have received unfettered access to economic opportunities across this continent for over 100 years. Now it is our turn!" This is what many call reverse discrimination.

Diversity education can overcome the reverse discrimination problem by showing employees the inclusive nature of the business case for equity. There is either equity for all or equity for none.

A diversity educational program must deal with any barrier to merit and fairness in the employment system. Merit can be thought of as the way the system treats the people. Fairness refers to the way people in the system treat other people. A diversity educational program therefore concentrates on doing away with the inequitable attitudes and systems that prevent a system from operating based on merit and fairness. But these barriers to merit and fairness do not affect only one, two, or four groups—they affect all employees.

The inclusive approach to equity will also handle the backlash issues of tokenism. Perhaps the biggest fear we encounter is voiced by members of minority groups—other than white males—who are concerned that they will be perceived as "tokens" in their organization because it is pursuing a diversity program. The inclusive approach advocated by a diversity program gets around this problem. No longer will members of the so-called designated groups feel that they are getting the job because of their gender and race, but now they can stand shoulder to shoulder with the white male who is requesting the very same goal, that is, an employment system based solely on merit and fairness for all.

Facing the Most Contentious Diversity Issues

It is difficult, if not impossible, to talk about issues of a diverse work force without evoking discussions of prejudice, discrimination, and workplace harassment. Needless to say, these are highly contentious and sometimes emotional issues that cannot be ignored if a diversity strategy is to be successful. A properly designed diversity educational program can provide a forum for a healthy discussion regarding these issues.

Not long ago, I was featured on a news magazine TV show. I was quoted as saying that "my mother is the biggest Archie Bunker I have ever met. She is incredibly racist and incredibly sexist."

After the broadcast I received a call from one of our clients, who was upset with my remarks. "How could you go on national television and call your mother racist and sexist?" she asked. I replied, "I was merely telling the truth. I wanted people to understand that white people do not have a monopoly on racism and men do not have a monopoly on sexism."

We all come out of a racist, sexist history. This was not something any of us asked for or even had any part in designing. But it is the reality that we were born into. In order for diversity issues to be discussed realistically, we must start by having some frank, truthful discussions about them. This is where diversity education can be most valuable.

Diversity education must answer the tough questions. What is sexism? What is racism? What is sexual harassment? What is gender harassment? Where do my stereotypes come from? Where do my prejudices come from? Do I discriminate? Is it wrong?

The best way to approach these issues is to invoke the no-guilt, no-blame, no-credit approach to diversity education. We must take no guilt or blame or credit for the way our society and organizations have evolved. Whatever happened in the past has happened and we can't change it. We need to acknowledge where we are on these issues today and commit to moving forward. This begins by having a frank and open discussion of the realities of prejudice, discrimination, and harassment in our work environments.

This is especially the case for issues of sexual harassment. Since the Thomas-Hill case, many people have started to demean the issue of sexual harassment by suggesting that harassment is about giving compliments and pulling out chairs for women. A properly designed diversity educational session can put this important issue in the proper context. Employees need to understand that harassment can ruin a person's life. Statistics show that a vast majority of women in the work force feel sexual harassment is a serious issue that damages workers by undermining confidence and impairing health.

Even a two-hour diversity training session can provide employees with a behavioural context for workplace harassment. Employees can understand the difference between acceptable, offensive, and illegal workplace behaviour by discussing the organization's workplace harassment policy. The policy outlines what is unacceptable in the work environment. An educational session should contain a discussion of the legal definition of harassment, the organization's policy, descriptions of behaviour that constitutes harassment, the specific procedure to handle workplace harassment, and the possible disciplinary procedures for confirmed cases.

Facing the highly contentious diversity issues is an important objective to be accomplished by diversity education. In order to do this, the organization will need to find skilled professionals to do the diversity training. Whether the trainers are internal or external, they must be competent facilitators who have a good information base and understand the dynamics of discussing these types of issues without evoking guilt and blame.

Identifying Attitudinal and Systemic Discrimination

One of the basic objectives of an effective educational program is to ensure that participants acknowledge that their employment system may not be operating based solely on merit and fairness. In other words, participants need to admit that their employment system may have been living a lie on the merit principle. This could be because of unfair attitudes or unfair systems.

Identifying the systemic barriers to merit will occur in the employment systems review (ESR). The results of the ESR can be fed back through the educational session. In the next chapter, we will talk about how to administer the employment systems review.

Systems sometimes do not operate according to merit because of unfair attitudes. These unfair attitudes are the famous "isms." The top ten famous isms are:

1. Sexism—discrimination based on sex/gender

2. Racism—discrimination based on race/colour

3. Ageism—discrimination based on being too old or too young

4. Haleism—discrimination based on disability

5. Credentialism—discrimination based on lack of education

6. Maternalism—discrimination based on family status

7. Nepotism—discrimination based on family association

8. Creedism—discrimination based on religion

9. Nationalism—discrimination based on national or cultural identity

10. Favouritism—discrimination based on fit to the old boys' or new girls' network

Attitudinally based discrimination can occur whenever a difference or perceived difference occurs in the workplace. The educational session is a good place to discuss these issues but it may be difficult to get participants to volunteer them. You will not be able to talk about attitudinal discrimination if people do not acknowledge that it exists.

Some organizations have used the diversity advisory committee to highlight unfair attitudes. Members of the advisory council conduct "spot interviews" in their respective areas of the company to determine which discrimination may be relevant. Each member is given a set of questions to guide the interviews. The results of the interviews are tallied and fed back to employees in the educational program. This allows participants to discuss attitudinal discrimination from a more objective perspective.

The following is a list of a typical set of DAC questions.

1. What initially attracted you to this company?

2. How do most employees find out about job openings here?

3. What does it take to be promoted here?

4. Do you think there is a shortage or surplus of good candidates within our company for management positions?

5. How often do you get performance appraisals?

6. How do you feel about development opportunities here?

7. Is training provided to high potential employees?

8. What could we do to make this company a better place to work?

9. Do you feel women and visible minorities with management potential are leaving our company?

10. What is your perception of our company vis-à-vis other companies regarding equitable treatment for all in the workplace?

To Introduce Participants to the Benefits of a Diverse Work Force

In light of the backlash issues mentioned earlier, it is not surprising that diversity is usually viewed from a negative perspective. The educational session is an opportunity to begin changing that perception. National Grocers has done this by ensuring that the educational session links into ways that store managers can improve their business by taking advantage of the diverse marketplace. Rob Rochon explains: "We ask the participants to take a look at their trading area and the demographics that make up their area. They then need to ask themselves 'What does this mean to my customer service strategies, our procurement strategies? How closely do the employees in my store reflect the trading area?' For example, if the ethnic community around a particular store is 35 percent of the population and the employees who represent the same community are only 2 percent, do we need to close the gap so that the store-employee mix resembles the market that it serves? How will that benefit us?

"We have also conducted focus groups with the ethnic communities that have and will continue to increase over the next decade. Based on current demographic projections, the selected target communities were Black/Caribbean, Southeast Asian, and Chinese. We asked them specifically about their shopping habits. Every group was concerned about price, but some groups were willing to trade off price for variety, quality, and service. Knowing what these consumers value helps store managers understand the local issues better and provide more effective customer service strategies.

"When you start engaging store managers in this manner, it breaks down resistance to new ways of doing business because they see the benefits. It also is a key contributor in shifting our culture to one that appreciates, understands, and supports diversity."

The National Grocers educational program shows specific benefits of valuing diversity. A proper educational program can allow participants to move past the more sensational issues surrounding diversity and look at the advantages inherent in a diverse work force.

Integrating the Quantitative and Qualitative Surveys

Many organizations use the educational session to administer both the quantitative and qualitative surveys that are part of the diversity program. This allows the organization to inform employees of the purpose of both surveys. It also allows the organization to have a higher rate of return on both surveys, which is especially important for the quantitative survey called the self-identification questionnaire (SIQ).

The self-identification questionnaire survey will be discussed in detail in Chapter 8. It is one element of the diversity strategy that is frequently misunderstood, miscommunicated, and consequently mishandled. One case involved an organization that had simply distributed the SIQ with no education and very little communication. More than 80 percent of employees did not return the questionnaire because they were so confused and outraged about its purpose. Those who did return the SIQ decided to add several sexist or racist comments to it such as "We should send women back home where they belong." The company could not use the information gathered in the process and had to repeat the whole exercise.

The organization had failed to educate its employees on why the information was being collected, where it would be stored, and who would have access to it. All of this can be conveyed in an educational session. Participants need to understand that the numbers collected in the SIQ will not be the focus of the diversity program but will be used as an oil light. Employees should be encouraged to review the SIQ form in the session and ask all the relevant questions there. After all the questions have been answered, participants can put their completed questionnaire in confidential envelopes that will go directly to the human resource department.

Employees also need to know that this information will not be put in their personnel file or be used in the employment decision. In one case, a young lawyer was looking for another job within a large law firm. She had filled out her SIQ many months before and submitted the information to the central human resource office. She began to realize that some of the interviewers had a copy of her SIQ when one senior partner in another division remarked about how interesting it was that she had descended from so many different racial groups. Needless to say, this applicant was very cautious about filling out future SIQs.

An organization can maximize the utility of the educational component of the equity program by including the administration of the SIQ. The administration of the survey in an education session allows an organization to collect the data effectively, address the tough questions, and ensure a high response rate.

SUMMARY

Achieving executive commitment and employee awareness and understanding are essential components of a properly designed diversity program. The executive group should be viewed as a special audience considering their level of responsibility to ensure that the diversity program is implemented in the organization. Given the demographic composition of the group it is likely that they will have had less first-hand experience with some of the more common diversity issues. Thus the presenter must anticipate reactions of ignorance, hostility, or apathy before an executive briefing is designed.

The communications and educational sessions go hand in hand to inform employees about the goal of the diversity program. Employees need to understand the business case and the reasons the organization is pursuing diversity. Participants also need to have an opportunity to discuss the realities of attitudinal and systemic discrimination within their employment systems. The educational sessions can also serve as an effective tool to administer the self-identification survey, which frequently generates confusion in the diversity program. Before being asked to complete it, participants need to understand why the information is being gathered, how it will be used, and where it will be stored.

We have included a suggested, generic outline for a diversity education session at the end of this chapter. This outline logically presents the diversity issues that should be covered during this stage. In Chapter 8 we have also included a copy of the SIQ form that should be used to collect quantitative data. This form will allow all employees to self-identify their status rather than identifying only members of the designated groups.

In the next chapter we will look at the importance of involving employees in the diversity program.

A Generic Outline for a Diversity Education Program

Introduction - Introduce participants, presenter, course objectives, and agenda.

Acknowledging Diversity - Allowing participants to link issues of diversity with equitable treatment in the workplace. This discussion should cover issues of gender, race, culture, class, religion, sexual orientation, family status, language, age, education, style, etc.

The Business Case for Equity - Define equity and equitable employment systems, introduce expectancy theory and the business case for equity, introduce the oil light to outline attitudinal and systemic discrimination.

The Age of Equity and Accommodation - Identify the Ages of Inequality, Equality, and Equity. Define accommodation and work through an accommodation case study.

Attitudinal Discrimination - Define stereotypes, prejudice, and discrimination. Work through the cycle of prejudice with participants.

Systemic Discrimination - Define systemic inequities in employment systems. Have participants determine which human resource policies and processes (formal and informal) are not consistent, accessible, and valid.

Gender Equity - Outline the various aspects of sexism in the workplace. Identify double standards between males and females in the organization.

Workplace Harassment - Legal definitions and prohibited grounds of harassment. Introduce the behavioural continuum. Review the organization's workplace harassment policy. Have participants complete case studies.

Call to Action - Have participants complete a self assessment tool to identify areas of improvement. Identify follow-up plans for next steps in the diversity strategy.

Assessments & Evaluations - Have participants complete course evaluations and feedback.

Chapter Seven

THE EMPLOYMENT SYSTEMS REVIEW:
HOW TO INVOLVE EMPLOYEES IN
DEVELOPING THE DIVERSITY STRATEGY

I n Chapter 4 we spoke about the need to have an inclusive diversity strategy, a strategy that moves past the perception that this initiative is for only four designated groups. This perception, created by legislated fairness programs, polarizes the employee base and results in an us-versus-them mentality once a program is introduced. The communications and education process outlined in the last chapter is an important component of creating inclusiveness. But in order for a program to be truly inclusive, the organization must go further than simply talking about it. A proper diversity program must actually demonstrate inclusiveness in its implementation.

Inclusiveness can be demonstrated by systematically involving employees from all parts of the organization. These employees will represent not just one priority group or four designated groups but the full spectrum of the organization's diversity. Every possible perspective of diversity should be considered—region, occupation, gender, race, culture, language, family status, age, sexual orientation, class, education, marital status, creed, etc. By involving employees from all backgrounds in the diversity strategy, the organization demonstrates the inclusive nature of the process, encouraging wider employee support for the initiative

and shifting an us-versus-them perspective to one that embod-
ies fairness for all.

In this chapter we will highlight the case of North American
Life Assurance Company (NAL). This company views diversity as
a key business issue and has oriented its products and services
to recognize and capitalize on the increasing diversity of the
Canadian mosaic. The CEO of the company, Brian Moore, recognizes that valuing diversity will strengthen how NAL intends to
conduct its business in an ever-changing market.

Janice Thomson, director of employment and staffing,
stressed that the success of the NAL diversity strategy was a direct
result of the quality and sequencing of events that accompanied
its launch. Ms. Thomson had already launched a diversity program in another organization and, because she knew where the
successes and pitfalls were, she capitalized on this experience to
ensure that the momentum of the NAL program continued.

NAL has gone to great lengths to ensure that its diversity
strategy is inclusive. The company did this by ensuring that all
its employees were actively involved with the corporate diversity initiative, starting at the design stage and continuing through
the implementation process.

One of the prime responsibilities Brian Moore charged NAL's
Equity Advisory Committee with was to conduct an employment
systems review. The employment system is made up of all the
policies and practices an organization uses to attract, select,
train, evaluate, promote, and compensate employees. The
employment system also establishes and defines jobs and determines the conditions of employment within the workplace. A
proper review of an employment system will identify barriers to
the fair treatment of recruitment, hiring, retention, promotion,
and treatment of employees.

THE EMPLOYMENT SYSTEMS REVIEW

One of the most important steps involving employees in the
development of the diversity strategy is in conducting an employment systems review (ESR). The ESR is an in-depth review of the
employment system, conducted with focus groups and interviews
with employees throughout the organization. It concentrates

primarily on finding and eliminating systemic discrimination in employment systems and is meant to be comprehensive and objective.

The two major objectives of an effective employment systems review are:

1. To examine all elements of the employment system, from hiring to termination, in order to identify and eliminate any elements that pose systemic barriers unrelated to merit.
2. Identify issues of favouritism and ensure consistency in policy and practice.

An essential element of the ESR is to ensure that there is consultation with employees. Consultation is necessary to protect the credibility of the review. It is important that members of the advisory committee conducting the review make no assumptions about inequity in the employment system. Thorough and comprehensive consultation will ensure that vital information is not overlooked by the advisory committee. Wide consultation ensures employees' willingness to participate in the entire diversity process and the eventual implementation of recommended changes.

Another important element of a proper ESR is to look at informal procedures in the employment process. Individuals from all levels should be asked to share their opinions and experiences about how things "really happen" in the organization. This means that the ESR must be conducted with a high degree of confidentiality and integrity. Thus the more people involved in the review, the better. If employees think the review is carried out by a lone individual or a select few, the entire process could be jeopardized.

NAL began its diversity journey by conducting organization-wide focus groups regarding the nature of the fairness in the employment system. Even though the organization had data from a previous employee opinion survey, it decided to conduct these diversity focus groups to increase employee involvement.

Once the feedback from the focus groups was analyzed, NAL decided to rework its original diversity strategy. It knew employees were looking to see if the information they had shared during the focus groups was reflected in the final plan. The organization felt that if employees found they were listened to, they would be more likely to support the diversity strategy when it was launched.

ESTABLISHING THE EQUITY ADVISORY COMMITTEE

Before actually conducting the employment systems review, it is necessary to establish an employee advisory committee. This advisory committee will conduct the employment systems review, be responsible for overseeing the presentation of the diversity strategy, and act as an important communications link to the employees. The representatives on the diversity advisory committee are themselves employees; therefore, the committee is yet another tool in enhancing employee involvement. The method used to establish the advisory committee must also be inclusive and epitomize fairness and inclusiveness. That is, it must allow every employee the opportunity to participate. How members of the committee get chosen is just as important as who gets chosen.

The method of establishing the equity advisory committee must be initiated by the champion in the organization. At NAL this body is called the Equity Advisory Committee. The objectives of the committee are to:

• Carry out the Employment Systems Review.

• Create short- and long-term diversity plans.

• Advise on communications throughout the organization.

• Serve as a "fairness committee" to suggest and react to policy changes.

• Develop preliminary budgets.

Brian Moore nominated himself as the key contact to the advisory committee because of his deep belief in the value of diversity to the business. Moore also agreed to chair an executive steering committee consisting of a cross-functional senior management group who works with the advisory committee. Its major functions are to:

- Approve annual plans and budgets for the diversity process.

- Approve long-term goals and timetables for the diversity strategy.

- Review the results of the employment systems review.

- Co-ordinate purchasing of outside training and survey services.

- Co-ordinate company-wide policy changes.

Members of the steering committee were chosen from a volunteer list of more than 55 executives from across NAL's key business functions and offices. Moore realized that the Strength in Diversity program needed to be driven by the top leaders within the organization with the support of the human resources department, not the other way around.

The process of selecting representatives for the employee advisory committee begins with communication from the champion regarding the need to establish the advisory committee. This communication can be a video, a notice on the bulletin board, or an article in the internal newspaper. Perhaps one of the most effective routes is a letter from the champion to each employee in the organization. This letter reinforces the importance of the diversity strategy, outlines the need for the advisory committee, identifies the process used to establish the committee, and requests volunteers. On the following page is a sample form that can be used to collect applications from employees interested in serving on the equity advisory committee.

It is important that the advisory committee members are seen as credible. Employees need to know who the members of the committee are and how they were chosen. Committee members must also be seen as knowledgeable and open to change. They will have to assure other employees that their input will make a difference and that they respect confidentiality. The advisory committee must establish a process that protects the input of other employees and publicizes it throughout the entire organization. Thomson explains, "NAL actually developed a communication network that has never been in place in an insurance company before. The fact that senior level executives were working alongside support employees to review, create, and write new policies sent a very powerful message to every NAL employee."

Name:_____

Office Telephone:_____

Location:_____

Report to:_____

Please respond to all of the following questions and return your completed application in complete confidence to:
Team Facilitator, Workplace Diversity, Human Resources Department, Head Office.

1. What does workplace diversity mean to you?

_____

_____

2. Since we are attempting to have a team of individuals with diverse personal attributes, we would appreciate information as follows. Please check the descriptors that apply to you:

❏ married   ❏ male

❏ married with children   ❏ female

❏ single   ❏ visible minority

❏ single parent   ❏ person with disability

❏ caring for aging dependant   ❏ Aboriginal person

                                            ❏ other (please explain)

Please describe any other relevant personal attributes you would bring to the team.

_____

_____

3. What would you like to achieve in your participation on this team?

_____

_____

_____

_____

4. Do you think you need training to be an effective team member?
             ❏ yes   ❏ no
If yes, what kind of training?

_____

_____

_____

5. What special skills and/or experience would you bring to this team?

_____

_____

Thomson advises that the advisory committee needs to communicate its accomplishments continually throughout the process. The committee has to accomplish recognizable developments that must be communicated to the employees weekly. Whether the development is a new logo, completion of a new piece of policy, or feedback on suggestions, it needs to be something that keeps diversity at the forefront. Thomson felt the communication of each step was a critical factor in the diversity plan being so well received by the employees.

"Everyone within NAL knew what was going on at relatively the same time. There were no secrets and everyone had input," she said. She emphasizes that it is critically important for organizations that implement diversity to maintain the momentum by aggressively communicating their initiatives to all employees. We covered the essential elements of an effective communications strategy in Chapter 6.

Once an advisory committee has been established, it should divide into a number of subcommittees to conduct the employment systems review. Each subcommittee is responsible for a separate element of the employment system. This division of responsibility allows the review process to proceed quickly and more efficiently than if the review is conducted by a single practitioner. Although the process is efficient, the subcommittee method requires time to compare results and recommendations to ensure consistency across the system.

Employment Systems Review Subcommittees

Eight subcommittees usually need to be established in the employment systems review, although smaller organizations may choose to form three subcommittees to look at selection, development, and conditions of employment. The recommended subcommittees for larger organizations will review

• Recruitment systems

• Selection systems

• Training and development systems

• Promotion systems

• Job evaluation systems

- Compensation and benefits systems

- Conditions of employment

- Performance systems (layoff, recall, disciplinary action, and termination)

Each subcommittee must review its portion of the employment system against six criteria.

1. Adverse impact (Does the policy or practice unfairly affect any given group?)

2. Job relatedness (Is the practice based on a bona-fide occupational requirement?)

3. Business necessity (Is the practice necessary for the safe and efficient operation of the business?)

4. Validity (Does the employment practice objectively measure what it was designed to measure?)

5. Consistency (Is the policy or procedure applied in a consistent manner to all personnel?)

6. Legality (Does the policy or practice conform to human rights and other legislation?)

Let us review the key issues to be considered by the subcommittees.

Reviewing the Recruitment Systems

An equitable employment system attracts the best-qualified candidates to fill employment opportunities. A company's recruitment process will determine how well its organization encourages or discourages applications from a wide pool of qualified candidates. When an organization is not attracting qualified candidates, it may be because it is using a biased recruitment system.

For example, when word-of-mouth recruitment is used to notify prospective applicants, only those who hear of the opening from families and friends of current employees will benefit. This may prevent an organization from broadening its pool of applicants.

The following questions should be answered by the subcommittee.

1. Are job postings and bulletin boards accessible to all employees, including those who work in branch offices or are physically challenged?

2. Are outreach recruitment strategies used to attract qualified prospective employees from a variety of communities?

3. Does the job poster accurately emphasize the qualifications and duties most central to the job?

4. Are skill components broken down to reflect actual job requirements?

5. Is someone who is familiar with the day-to-day functions of the job available to provide prospective applicants with information?

6. Is the language used in job postings and advertisements checked for gender- and culture-neutral language?

7. Is "experience" asked for instead of "Canadian experience" or "university education or equivalent" rather than "degree from a Canadian university"?

8. Is illustrated material used in recruiting checked for gender and cultural biases?

9. Have personnel staff received training with respect to human-rights and other employment-related legislation?

10. Have up-to-date human rights and other relevant legislation and information been used in preparing your company's job application form?

11. Is the personnel department accessible to people with physical disabilities?

12. Do job descriptions/advertisements specify the physical requirements of the job based on a physical-demands analysis?

The review of the recruitment system must deal with internal as well as external recruitment practices. Many organizations ignore the systemic bias of internal word-of-mouth referral systems. These informal systems can significantly limit reaching the most qualified candidates within an organization. One way to avoid this is to design a comprehensive employee skills inventory. Such an inventory lists the transferable skills of each employee in the organization—for example, the ability to speak other languages. It is compiled when employees complete a generic questionnaire that requests information on occupational experience, general and technical knowledge, physical and mental ability, and educational credentials. This skills inventory, if kept up to date, can be used to identify possible candidates within an organization for job openings.

One of the most difficult barriers to equitable recruitment is the seniority-based system, which can occur even without a union. In organizations where this practice exists, it is usually referred to as entitlement programs. When seniority is perceived as a barrier to fair recruitment, it is important for the advisory committee to work with representatives of the union, if there is one, to develop co-operative solutions to ensure hiring is merit-based.

Reviewing the Selection Systems

The selection system is the process of choosing the right candidate for a given job. In order to draw up criteria for choosing the right candidate, the subcommittee must have a good understanding of what the job requires. These criteria are what is referred to as "bona fide" job requirements.

Selection methods directly affect the quality of an organization's work force. When subjective and non-job-related criteria are used in the selection process, barriers to equity may exist. These barriers will discriminate against some qualified applicants within or outside of an organization's work force.

Here are some examples of bias in selection systems.

• Many companies today favour applicants who have university degrees even though the job does not require the credential.

• Many employment interviews do not use standardized questions, thus creating difficulty in comparing the interview results of each candidate. The interviews have an inconsistent format, which tends to encourage subjective assessments.

- Some interviewers may not be sensitive to cultural differences that could cause breakdowns in communication because of a misinterpretation of verbal and non-verbal signals.

- Interviewers look for candidates who exhibit characteristics that they themselves exhibit.

The subcommittee must review all elements of the selection process such as paper screening, the testing process, the interviewing process, and reference checks. The subcommittee should ask the following questions when reviewing the selection system.

1. Are front-line staff and interviewers familiar with human rights and other employment-related legislation?

2. Are managers and interviewers aware of the organization's diversity philosophy and goals?

3. Is the selection process, including interviews, fully documented?

4. Are tests validated for job-relatedness?

5. Are tests examined for gender and racial biases?

6. Are tests administered by trained personnel?

7. Are testing conditions standardized?

8. Is the testing facility accessible to wheelchair users?

9. Are procedures for reference checks standardized?

The interview process frequently includes forms of unintentional discrimination merely because of how a question is phrased.

Reviewing the Training and Development Systems

Training and development systems are meant to provide employees with opportunities to improve their performance in their existing jobs and acquire additional skills for future opportunities. Training usually refers to more formal components of skills development. Development refers to opportunities to develop skills through secondments, and temporary and rotational assignments.

Organizations can offer several training and development opportunities. The more traditional approaches include

- On-the-job training

- Institutional training

- Apprenticeship training

- Career development assignments

- Job rotations

- In-house training courses

- Subsidized educational leaves of absence

- Bridging programs

- Internships

When inequity occurs in training and development practices, there is a direct impact on employee development. Poor employee development leads to job ghettos where employees are stifled in positions for long periods of time because they lack the necessary qualifications to move on. A proper review of the training and development systems will include a review of the internal recruitment and mobility systems.

The following questions should be asked by the subcommittee.

1. Does the organization have a training and development policy based on fair principles?

2. Are all employees aware of the organization's training and development opportunities?

3. Do all employees have access to training and development opportunities?

4. Has the organization ensured that there are no restrictions to training opportunities based on occupational levels and earnings?

5. Do employees have access to in-house or company-paid career counselling?

A common characteristic of most training and development systems is that they concentrate on opportunities for employees in the higher levels in an organization. Rarely are the same training and development opportunities provided to administrative or clerical workers. One way to overcome this is to develop or revise the training and development policy to allow access to the broadest pool of employees possible.

A proper training and development policy should

- State that eligibility criteria must be written in terms of the skills required for a training course, not the level within the organization.

- Be easy to understand.

- Reflect the participation of all employees at all levels of the organization.

- Be well communicated to all employees through the orientation process and regular channels.

- Be supported by all managers and supervisors to ensure they make training and development opportunities available to all employees.

Once an organization has established a training and development policy, it will be necessary to assess how effective the policy has been. The organization does this by monitoring enrolment in training programs. If enrolments are low, the organization will need to establish the causes and remove them.

Reviewing the Promotion System

The mobility system in an organization should be designed to ensure the promotion of the best candidates to higher positions in the organization. This part of the employment system also helps employees define and acquire the skills and experience they need for promotion.

We have yet to meet an executive group that is not convinced that their organization's promotion system is based on the merit principle. However, when you ask their employees, you hear a different story. Some employees will tell you that the seniority system gets in the way of merit because the newer hires have no chance of advancement. Others will say that the promotion system is a secretive process dominated by the whims of senior management. Still other employees feel that promotion is based solely on favouritism and an employee's willingness not to "rock the boat" in the organization. Whatever the reason, promotion based solely on merit rarely exists.

A properly designed upward mobility system will:

- Emphasize the potential of candidates as well as actual skills and talents.

- Use the existing internal work force to fill positions as well as external recruitment.

- Have a well-developed career-counselling program.

- Have a widely accessible training and development program.

- Use a number of methods to help people gain the experience and skills needed for promotion.

- Be closely monitored to ensure benefit to all employees.

The subcommittee reviewing the promotion system will run into very similar issues identified by the recruitment committee. The criteria for recruitment should be reflected in the promotion system. A review of the organization's promotion system begins with an objective analysis of how promotions have operated in the recent past.

A good place to start is to examine data on promotions within the organization over the past five years. The human resource department should be able to provide much of this information in aggregate form so that no individual can be identified. When anonymity is not possible—for example, in very senior positions—confidential information such as salary data should not be collected.

A proper review of the promotion system will look at the positions people have come from as well as the positions they have gone to. Charting the flow of personnel through the organization will point out common career paths. This review may also bring to the fore inconsistencies in the process.

The subcommittee conducting the review must be able to identify which occupations and what areas of the organization are most likely to produce future managers based on past performance of the system. The review will also uncover those career paths that lead to "dead-end" jobs and the types of people who wind up on such a path. This review will frequently uncover "job ghettos" for women, minorities, or elderly workers. These are jobs where one particular group is concentrated and where most of this group's career path leads—for example, an over-representation of females in human resources. Job ghettos are a reliable signal that some form of systemic discrimination exists in the organization.

The analysis of the quantitative data surrounding the promotional system should be coupled with qualitative data from interviews and focus groups. Individuals in higher positions in the organization can be surveyed to find out the "soft" information regarding the workings of the promotional system. Senior people will be able to explain how they got to their current position, the development opportunities they had along the way, and how they were mentored in the process. Their experiences will confirm the picture being painted by the quantitative review.

The subcommittee reviewing this part of the employment system should consider the following questions:

1. Are there identified formal lines of progression or career paths for each occupational group and each employee?

2. Has this information been made available to all employees as part of a career-counselling or performance-appraisal session?

3. Are there entry level jobs in each job category from which employees have the opportunity to advance?

4. Are there established criteria to select employees for upward-mobility opportunities?

5. Are the criteria based on knowledge and skill requirements and not on occupational level or having a certain background?

6. Is there an appropriate information package and communication strategy to publicize mobility initiatives and selection
   procedures?

7. Is a variety of upward-mobility opportunities used to ensure
   equitable promotion for all employees?

Reviewing the Job Evaluation System

The job evaluation system is a process used to determine the relative worth of jobs in an organization. Many job evaluation
reviews were conducted as part of an organization's pay equity
program. Such a review helps an organization to identify how
each job should be compensated.

The job evaluation system involves defining the specific
tasks and duties of a job and the skills required to perform it.
Thus job evaluation becomes an important basis for other
employment decisions such as recruitment, selection, training,
and compensation.

A proper job evaluation systems review involves three steps:

1. Job analysis.

2. Job evaluation.

3. Establishment of pay rate.

The first step, the job analysis, reviews the responsibilities of
the job, the skills and knowledge required, the effort required,
and the working conditions. The analysis must go past a simple
review of job descriptions since they could be out of date or
incomplete. It should include an objective observation of competent workers actually performing the job. These data can be
supplemented with information from managers and supervisors.

The second step is to conduct a proper job evaluation. With
the knowledge gained from the job analysis, the relative worth of
a job is assessed. There are several methods to conduct a job
evaluation review. A proper evaluation must look at a job's ranking, classification, point system, and factor comparison.

Jobs are ranked from the least complex to the most complex
and from lowest to highest level of responsibility. It is likely that
the ranking will be based on subjective opinion, so it is important

to include several committee members to obtain a wider perspective on the rankings.

The factor classification of a job uses market value (i.e., what other companies pay a person in the same position) to determine a job's worth. To determine the market value of the job many organizations start with a point system, which assigns points to specific job factors such as responsibility and skill. These points can be broken down into sub-points to create a more accurate picture for the job. This will allow the subcommittee to move to the final stage, the establishment of the pay rate. Key jobs are evaluated and ranked according to factors such as skills, responsibilities, working conditions, and effort. The current salary for each key job is divided so that each job factor has an ascribed dollar value. This becomes the basis for evaluating remaining jobs. Relative worth is indicated by a job's wage rate.

Job grading or classification involves grouping jobs into the specific grades and then ranking them in terms of difficulty or level of responsibility. Here again, this system is probably based on subjective opinion and requires several reviewers.

To determine a fair rate of pay, most companies use wage and salary surveys of what other employers in the same labour market are paying.

The job evaluation subcommittee must consider the following questions in their review:

1. Does the job analysis process involve interviews with workers and supervisors to collect information, as opposed to relying strictly on job descriptions?

2. Are jobs evaluated on the basis of established, objective criteria and not on subjective opinion?

3. Does your organization have job descriptions for each position and do they accurately reflect the jobs to which they pertain?

4. Are wages in your organization based on surveys from sources that have already reviewed and adjusted salaries for comparable worth and equal pay?

5. Are job evaluations completed by more than one person?

6. Has the job evaluation subcommittee received awareness training to understand systemic discrimination issues?

7. Does your subcommittee represent various occupational groups?

Reviewing the Compensation and Benefits Systems

Salary and benefits together form the total compensation package for employees. Compensation is payment that may consist of salary, wages, commissions, and bonuses but that must also include benefits. Benefits may include paid vacation, insurance plans, pension plans, RRSPs, expense accounts, company car, educational allowances, and stock options. A properly designed compensation system will attract, retain, motivate, and pay an employee for services rendered.

How much a person is paid to perform these services can be influenced by several subjective factors such as social bias of market value, the applicant's perceived need to work, and the employee's ability to negotiate a raise. Thus it is important that the committee use as many objective assessments of the compensation system as possible. Objective assessments include market value and pay equity comparisons.

Job evaluation, recruitment and selection practices, training and development practices and promotional systems all affect compensation. After jobs have been ranked, an organization can determine the formal and informal methods of compensation. The company's policies, practices, and collective agreements that govern compensation should be examined.

The compensation review also needs to determine the process for salary increments. These increments are sometimes based on performance or "merit." But many times a raise in pay is based on "bell-curving" the performance to ensure that the increments remain within budget. When employees are ranked against one another to determine merit, performance criteria are usually not consistent. Employees will figure out how the compensation system really works and realize the inequity of bell-curving salary increases, and, as a result, will reduce their effort.

Once inequities in a pay system are identified, corrections can be made by providing salary adjustments for individuals or groups who are unfairly compensated, using flat raises to replace percentage-based raises, and reassessing jobs to establish equal worth and to adjust pay accordingly.

The benefits system is a bit more difficult to evaluate than the salary portion of the compensation system. Some benefits may not be available to all employees due to eligibility criteria. But the committee should ensure that the eligibility criteria being used for benefits and perks are equitably exclusionary. The committee should also pay particular attention to the availability of benefits for part-time workers.

The most common inequities in the benefits system are found in maternity or child-care leave. Employees who take such leave may be penalized by the interruption of their benefit payments, including pension contributions. Another inequity relates to lack of recognition for non-majority religious holidays. Failure to grant paid leave or unpaid leave for these days could be viewed by a human rights commission as a breach of the employer's duty to accommodate.

The compensation subcommittee must ask the following questions in a review:

1. Has the organization completed a statistical review of compensation rates according to department and occupation?

2. Is the organization's compensation system based on principles of equal pay?

3. Have pay ranges been established for all jobs?

4. Are pay ranges based on the value the organization places on the job and not on market value?

5. Have recruitment and selection procedures been reviewed for their impact on compensation?

6. Are the organization's pay scales publicized or accessible to employees?

7. Are existing pay differentials based on such factors as skill, effort, responsibility, and working conditions and not on irrelevant factors such as gender or race?

8. Is the organization's method of determining merit pay consistently applied?

9. If wage discrepancies have been noted, is there a plan of action to change procedures and equalize the pay of those affected?

10. Are requests for non-majority holidays accommodated?

11. Do women who take maternity or child care leave have access to full benefits?

12. Are benefits available to part-time, seasonal, casual, and temporary workers?

13. If there are benefit differentials, are they based on legitimate job requirements?

14. Are employees aware of all benefits available to them?

Reviewing Working Conditions

Working conditions refers to the physical and social environment of a workplace. Working conditions are governed by the policies and practices that regulate work sites and workers. The committee reviewing this part of an employment system needs to look at policies surrounding health and safety, dress code, attendance, flexible work arrangements, family care, and harassment. Companies that do not ensure a hospitable working environment for all employees tend to experience problems with worker satisfaction, low productivity, and high turnover. They may also be vulnerable to human rights complaints.

The most important part of the working conditions review is to ensure that the work environment is free from harassment and discrimination. These behaviours create a negative work environment and contribute to lower productivity. One major employer who has researched the effects of harassment in its workplace has found that over more than 780 hours were lost each time a harassment issue surfaced. These hours were used in short-term disability leaves, counselling sessions, and time spent during investigations.

Today harassment has become a major management issue due to media coverage. Employees are more aware that they have a right to be free from harassment and discrimination in the workplace. The working conditions subcommittee needs to establish if the organization has created such an environment and if not, what more needs to be done. Reducing harassment and discrimination will require a proactive approach beginning with the design of an effective policy. This must be followed by extensive communication and education regarding the complaint process and disciplinary action for perpetrators.

The questions to be considered by this subcommittee are:

1. Does the organization provide reliable security, health, and safety measures to ensure the safety of all employees?

2. Are formal and informal dress codes in accordance with human rights legislation and are they job-related?

3. Are dress codes enforced consistently throughout the organization?

4. Does the organization offer flexible work arrangements, such as part-time work, flexible hours, or alternative workplace locations?

5. Does the organization recognize child- and elder-care needs in its leave policies?

6. Does your company have a workplace harassment/discrimination policy that is understood by all employees?

7. Do all employees clearly understand what is acceptable and unacceptable behaviour?

8. When formal harassment/discrimination complaints are filed, are they followed up quickly and confidentially?

9. Have management and supervisory teams had training to identify and deal with harassment issues in the workplace?

Reviewing the Performance System

Layoff, recall, disciplinary action, and termination are employer-initiated actions in response to factors related to poor employee performance and insubordination. A review of these elements of the employment system must pay particular attention to the adverse impact on specific groups and the consistency of their use.

Start with a review of the policies pertaining to these areas of the employment system. Look at how the performance-appraisal process is used in making layoff or termination decisions. Consistently using performance appraisals can ensure that significant personnel decisions are based on objective, documented criteria. But these performance appraisals themselves must be based on objective, job-related criteria rather than subjective opinion.

The other major part of the performance system that must be reviewed is the discipline system. All employees must be fully aware of the values of the organization, the expectations of the employer, and the consequences of not performing. When an employee breaks the rules of an organization, he or she must know what the penalty will be. This penalty could include warnings, suspensions without pay, and ultimately termination. It is important that some policy exist to ensure that these penalties are not used casually by management.

The most drastic disciplinary action is termination of an employee. Many organizations have a termination policy but it may be poorly communicated and therefore poorly understood. More specifically, warning and punitive procedures are often outlined in general terms that are too vague for employees to understand. The committee must examine termination records and exit interviews to determine the fairness of the termination process.

The performance systems subcommittee must ask the following questions:

1. Does the organization have policies in place for layoff, disciplinary action, and termination?

2. Are discipline, layoff, and termination decisions based on clearly defined, job-related, and objective criteria?

3. Have the company's employees been provided with information on the organization's policies and procedures for layoff, discipline, and termination?

4. Does management in the company follow an established procedure when taking disciplinary action against an employee?

5. Are formal exit interviews conducted to determine the reasons for voluntary employee terminations?

CONCLUSION

One of the most important requirements of an effective diversity strategy is that it be inclusive of all employees. The best way to ensure inclusiveness is to systematically involve all employees in the strategy. Involving employees ensures that there is a strong commitment for the initiatives pursued in the diversity strategy.

The employment systems review is an effective vehicle for employee envolvement. An effective ESR will allow for the participation of many employees who will be given the responsibility of objectively identifying systemic discrimination. The employees reviewing the various parts of the employment system can ensure that policies and procedures in the organization meet the criteria of consistency, accessibility, job-relatedness, validity, legality, and equitable impact.

In the next chapter we will discuss how to measure more variable factors, such as employee attitudes, in the employment systems.

Chapter Eight

EFFECTIVE MEASUREMENT IN A DIVERSITY STRATEGY

I n Chapter 4 we stated that the heart of a proper diversity strategy is effective measurement. We outlined that legislated fairness programs concentrated on the measurement of the representation of members of designated groups. While representation numbers may signal inequity in a system, they will tell little about the actual degree of inequity. How does an organization consistently and reliably measure fairness?

In this chapter we will outline various ways to measure equity in an employment system. Most of these measures are qualitative, based on employee perception. However, an effective diversity program will also include quantitative measurement of representation data. We will show how the accurate measurement of employee perception along with an analysis of representation data can provide the basis for action in a diversity program. We will also see how the employees' perception of fairness adds credibility to the information gleaned from the employment systems review.

THE SELF-IDENTIFICATION
QUESTIONNAIRE (SIQ)

The major tool to gather quantitative information is the self-identification questionnaire (SIQ). This instrument allows an organization to conduct a census of the internal representation of various groups by occupational category. We have included a copy of a standard SIQ form that is used to collect quantitative data.

Private and Confidential   *Omnibus Consulting Inc.*

Employment Equity Questionnaire

Surname/First Name/Initial(s) | Employee No. | Sex | Division/Group

M F

1 A number of groups that comprise the Canadian population are listed below.
Please check the one box that best describes your origin: (We are not seeking information on nationality or religion)

Black *(eg. Africa, Canada, United States, West Indies, other blacks)* ❑

Canadian Aboriginal
Inuit ❑   Non-Status Indian ❑   Metis ❑   Status Indian ❑

Chinese ❑   Japanese ❑   Korean ❑

Indo-Pakistani *(e.g. Bangladesh, India, Pakistan, Sri Lanka)* ❑

Oceanic *(e.g. Melanesia, Micronesia, Polynesia)* ❑

South Asian *(e.g. Cambodia/Kampuchea, Laos, Malaysia, Myanmar, Philippines, Thailand, Vietnam)* ❑

West Asian or Arab *(e.g. Afghanistan, Armenia, Egypt, Iran, Iraq, Jordan, Lebanon, Syria)* ❑

White *(e.g. Canada, Europe, Great Britain, Ireland,
Latin/South America of Caucasian background, Russia, United States)* ❑

Other *(e.g. mixed racial origin)* specify.. ❑

2 If you have any loss or abnormality of psychological, physiological or anatomical structure or function that limits at least one of your major activities, please check the applicable box or boxes.

Blindness/severe visual impairment not correctable by glasses/contact lenses *(e.g. astigmatism, glaucoma)* ❑ | Muteness/speech impairment *(e.g. aphasia)* ❑
Coordination/dexterity impairment *(e.g. arthritis, cerebral palsy, cystic fibrosis, multiple sclerosis)* ❑ | Non-visible physical impairment *(e.g. allergies, asthma, back problems, epilepsy, hemophilia)* ❑
Deafness/hearing impairment ❑ | Mental Illness/severe personality disorder *(e.g. schizophrenia)* ❑
Developmental/mental deficiency *(e.g. dyslexia)* ❑ |
Mobility/capability impairment *(e.g. amputations, dwarfism, paraplegia)* ❑ | Visual impairment correctable by glasses/contact lenses *(long or short sightedness)* ❑
Other impairment (specify) .... ❑

I do not wish to complete this questionnaire. ❑

Comments..

Signature .... Date ....

*Thank you for your cooperation.
Please enclose the survey in the envelope provided.*
© Copyright 1990 *Omnibus Consulting Inc.*

Before conducting the quantitative survey with the SIQ, an organization should inform employees about the purpose of the survey. Employees should also be advised that completing the questionnaire is voluntary and that the information collected will not appear on their personnel files. It can be beneficial to include a statement of confidentiality with the SIQ. This statement will outline how the information will be used, who will have access to it, and when it will be updated or destroyed.

In order to get a valid measurement of representation within a work force, every effort should be made to have each employee complete the SIQ. In order to achieve a 100 percent response rate, the organization needs to have a strong communication strategy that answers some of the most common questions about the SIQ. Let us review some of these questions.

Common Questions and Answers Regarding the SIQ

Q) What is the purpose of the self-identification questionnaire?

A) The SIQ is a type of census that allows us to determine whether our diversity initiatives are working effectively and will allow us to measure success over the years.

Q) Why do you ask employees to provide their names and employee number on the SIQ?

A) We need to be able to track the employment status of all individuals over time. We can track only by identifying an employee's occupational code, which along with an employee's specific information can be accessed only by the employee's number. Once the employee has been identified, we can determine the specific occupational category of each respondent. This information can be compared to the corresponding occupational category in the wider work force.

Q) Is the SIQ voluntary?

A) Yes, it is. However, it is vital that each employee complete the survey so that our data base is accurate and complete. This is information that only the employee can provide. The data will be held in the strictest confidence, stored separately from your personnel file, and used for the sole purpose of aggregate reporting.

Q) Who will have access to this information?

A) Access will be limited to a small number of human resource profes-sionals whose specific responsibilities deal with diversity initiatives.

Q) Why has the company decided to ask employees to self-identify rather than having managers provide this informa-tion?

A) First of all, we want employees to understand what we are doing and why we are doing it. The best way of achieving this is to have them be a part of the data-gathering process. Second, only employees can accu-rately and consistently identify themselves. The opinion of another per-son as to what race the employee belongs is subjective, error-prone, and irrelevant. In the case of disabled employees, there are many dis-abilities that are not visible. Therefore, only the employee is knowl-edgeable and able to self-identify.

Q) Is it likely that members of some groups will receive pref-erential treatment as a result of information gathered in this survey?

A) Our policy has always been to hire and promote the best candidate for the job based on the job-related qualifications and merit. We have no intention of changing this policy. After reviewing this information, we may find that qualified people from certain groups are not applying for jobs in our company for various reasons. We can then address this problem in a specific equity initiative, like more aggressive outreach.

Q) Aren't there questions that employers are not supposed to ask under the Human Rights Act?

A) While some questions would not be acceptable to ask *before* mak-ing a decision to hire an individual, an employer can ask the questions of people once they become employees. In fact, the Human Rights Commission endorses the collection of such information as long as it is used for an equity-related program like ours.

Q) What about the question of reverse discrimination?

A) Certainly, some employees may feel threatened by our diversity ini-tiative. However, it is important to remember that the foundation of the policy is the strengthening and reinforcement of the merit principle. This information will be combined with qualitative information gathered from attitude surveys that will guide the diversity program.

Answering these types of questions can be done by combining the SIQ with an educational session. This will allow employees the opportunity to complete the SIQ while being updated on its purpose, a topic covered in more detail in the next chapter.

While quantitative data are important to an effective diversity strategy, they must not be the focus. The most important information to be gathered is qualitative data. These data determine the perception of fairness by employees. Let us look at how they can be collected.

MEASURING EQUITY

In an earlier chapter, we discussed how inequity manifests itself in an organization. Inequity can exist because the system treats employees unfairly. This is called systemic discrimination. Inequity can also exist when people in the system treat others unfairly. This is called attitudinal discrimination. In the last chapter, we saw how the employment systems review is designed to identify forms of systemic discrimination. We will now see how to root out forms of attitudinal discrimination by measuring employee perceptions.

Measuring Employee Perceptions

One challenge of the vision of getting to a Five is to know how you are doing in your quest to achieve the goal. The employment system review discussed in the last chapter will provide a partial answer to this question. But the real way to know is to ask an expert. An organization needs to find the twenty-first century equivalent of the Delphic Oracle. And interestingly enough, the search is not as complex as you might think. You are surrounded by experts in fairness. They are the people who operate in the employment system—the employees. Employees are the ones who know how the employment system treats people. Measuring these perceptions can be the basis for future action in a diversity strategy.

There are at least four major ways to measure employee perceptions for a diversity strategy. They are:

1. Informal and structured interviews.

2. Focus groups.

3. Non-normed climate surveys.

4. Normed opinion surveys.

Let us consider the value of each.

Informal and Structured Interviews

One of the most basic approaches to gathering employee perceptions is to conduct employee interviews. These interviews
can range from informal, casual conversations in the lunchroom
to more formal conversations in office meetings. They can be
conducted by either internal or external objective facilitators.

Conversation and interviews will elicit anecdotal information about the personnel process and reflect the inequitable attitudes that may be experienced by staff. For example, we
conducted one interview around a cafeteria table in one organization. We asked the general question "What is it like to work
around here?" The response produced stories about everything
from reverse discrimination to management insensitivity to
harassment concerns. One employee spoke about the inability
of visible minorities to move past the glass ceiling regardless of
their academic qualifications. It was pretty obvious that this
group of employees felt the employment system was less than
equitable.

The interview approach invariably produces anecdotes and
information that can be used by champions of the diversity
strategy to help advance the cause. This information can certainly affect any member of the senior management group who
may be wavering in his or her commitment to support the diversity program.

The problem with this approach is that it lacks scientific consistency, reliability, and replicability. The interviews will reflect
the feelings of only certain employees at that particular time. It
will be only a brief snapshot of employee perception, not a comprehensive overview. Also, depending on who is conducting the
interviews, the information may reflect what the employee
thinks the interviewer wants to hear.

The most important problem with this approach is that it
will be difficult to synthesize the information from the process.
Feedback is likely to be highly subjective, not based on fact and

possibly tainted by emotion. Thus it will be difficult to replicate the process in the future, an essential part in determining progress in a diversity strategy. Thus an organization needs a more scientific approach to gathering employee perceptions.

Focus Groups

Focus groups represent a somewhat more disciplined approach to the qualitative measurement problem. Employees are chosen at random from across the organization and grouped into defined categories. These categories could be gender, status, division, race, or occupational classifications. Each group is asked the same set of prepared questions. The advantage of the focus group is that it is a more reliable approach to gathering employee perceptions than unstructured interviews because the same questions are asked of all focus groups. Also, the sample is randomly chosen, reducing the possibility of bias. Furthermore, focus groups can be chosen to reflect the current employee mix in an organization.

For example, a recent focus group of women in a financial services company was discussing what it would take for one of them to become a vice-president. At that time, all incumbents were men. A number of the women told about their use of the company's relatively new self-managed career-development program. This was a state-of-the-art initiative with close links to the performance management system, individual development planning with budgets and contracts, mentoring, tuition refunds, etc. After listening to the praise for the program, one of the two Asian women in the group stated that the program may be great but it wouldn't work for them. They pointed out that their culture was based on passivity, in waiting to be asked, and, for women, on deference to men. The program, based on mainstream North American business values, was strong on self-promotion and "grabbing the brass ring." With almost one-fifth of the work force of Asian background, the organization realized that it needed to review this aspect of the career-development process.

The limitation of the focus group approach is that it is also based on highly subjective comments that can be emotionally charged. Thus it can be hard to determine exactly what the feedback means because the information is not compared to anything other than the perception of other groups in the system.

The focus group approach also provides only a snapshot of employee perceptions. It may provide enough information to convince the executive to launch a diversity program but will not be enough to determine progress. That is, focus group information will not provide enough factual information to measure the extent to which your initiatives are moving towards your diversity goals. This is because, as with any snapshot, you really cannot take the same picture twice.

Furthermore, focus groups are more confidential than group interviews but they are not anonymous. It would still be possible to determine which employees participated in the focus group even though they were randomly chosen. This could inhibit the participation of employees or affect their willingness to provide honest feedback. In order to ensure complete confidentiality, an organization would have to turn to a more anonymous approach to gathering information.

Non-Normed Climate Surveys

A non-normed climate survey is an anonymous assessment of employee perception in an organization. These instruments will be more reliable than focus groups because every employee has a chance to respond and there is little fear of being identified. Non-normed surveys are imports from market research techniques and they are meant to measure what is going on now in the organization.

One organization we have worked with conducted a non-normed climate survey with more than 6,000 employees. The objective of the survey was to obtain opinions from employees on issues relating to diversity within the organization. The results were compared to the overall response population as well as breakdowns by location; management groupings; union versus non-union; and full-, part-time, and contract employment status. In addition, the organization looked at employees' results according to whether they belonged to one of four groups— women, racial minorities, persons with disabilities, and Aboriginal people.

The organization received a response rate of over 40 percent with more than 2,600 employees completing and returning the survey. The survey uncovered several inconsistencies in employee perception of fairness within the organization. For example, employees with disabilities reported significantly lower perceptions of job satisfaction than the overall employee population. The survey also showed that a lower percentage of contract workers felt they were recognized for a job well done than the overall employee participation. This information gave the organization an opportunity to determine the priorities in their diversity strategy and provided important information to supplement the employment systems review. An example of the type of non-normed instrument used is reproduced below.

A sample of a non-normed questionnaire to identify key diversity issues.

The following questions are answered on a scale of 1 to 5.
1 - **Strongly Disagree,** 2 - **Disagree,** 3 - **Neither Agree nor Disagree,** 4 - **Agree,** and 5 - **Strongly Agree**

1. I am aware of the goals and principles of my organization's diversity strategy.

2. I feel the diversity program could create reverse discrimination.

3. It would be valuable to have an internal Human Rights Workplace Harassment Program in our organization.

4. I would make use of an internal Human Rights Workplace Harassment Program if I needed to.

5. My boss treats everyone fairly.

6. Getting ahead in our organization is based on "who you know."

7. I feel I am recognized for a job well done.

8. I have difficulty accepting a boss who is:

    (a) a woman

    (b) a visible minority

(c) has a disability

(d) a white male

9. I am satisfied with the information I receive about what is going on in the company.

10. I feel a more diverse work force would be disruptive to operations at the company.

11. I expect to make more progress in my job than I have up until now.

12. The company cares about my work more than it cares about me.

13. My job gives me the chance to learn new skills.

14. I have the chance to get a better job at the company.

15. The company does not provide me with enough information to do my job well.

16. I get a real sense of achievement from my work.

17. Canada should have two official languages—French and English.

18. Women promoted into management supervisory positions are treated with equal respect to men.

19. I believe the following groups have an equal opportunity for employment in this company:

    (a) women

    (b) visible minorities

    (c) people with disabilities

    (d) white males

20. This company has done more than it should to provide equitable opportunities for

    (a) women

    (b) people with disabilities

    (c) visible minorities

    (d) white males

There are also restrictions to the non-normed approach. The first problem is that it is, again, simply a snapshot in time. As such it is not easily replicated and thus cannot be used to accurately measure progress over time. Second, the information does not provide comparative data. An organization will have no way to determine how fair it may be compared to others in its industry because the instrument is designed for use by that particular organization.

Nevertheless, up until now many organizations have taken the non-normed approach to employee assessment because they have had no other choice. These organizations soon discover, however, that repeat applications of the survey cannot be validly and reliably compared to earlier results. The real tragedy is that such surveys usually cost about the same as a normed instrument, which would allow a ready comparison to others in the industry and can be replicated over time in order to measure progress. However, up until now a fully normed instrument that consistently and reliably measures equity has not been available in North America.

THE EQUITY QUOTIENT— A NORMED OPINION SURVEY

On January 26, 1995, at a breakfast meeting at the prestigious Royal York Hotel in Toronto, representatives of 75 major Canadian organizations were introduced to a dramatically different approach to the measurement of fairness in the workplace. The approach was a fully normed opinion survey called "The Equity Quotient."

This impressive new instrument would allow organizations, for the first time, to measure employee perceptions of fairness compared to established Canadian norms. Any question on an attitude survey is considered to be normed when it has been asked repeatedly of employees in several organizations. When the question has been asked enough times, the question becomes a norm. An organizational norm is sturdy enough to serve as a standard for the industry. To qualify as an organizational norm, a particular question has to be asked of and answered by employees in at least 10 organizations and from a sample base of at least 1,000 respondents. A strong normed question will have been asked and answered in at least 100 organizations to more than 80,000 respondents.

The Equity Quotient (EQ) was invented by Dr. Gail Cook Johnson. Dr. Johnson is a former Chief Statistician of Canada on the Advisory Committee for Labour Statistics and holds a doctorate in Business Administration specializing in Organizational Development and Industrial Relations from the Sloan School of Management at Massachusetts Institute of Technology.

She describes the EQ as a sophisticated instrument that is the result of extensive research and that can be used to measure reliably and consistently the perception of fairness in the workplace. Johnson states: "The EQ encourages a model of diversity which is based on the ability to canvass the opinions of employees using a very sophisticated approach to the collection and understanding of employee opinions and attitudes to measure their perceptions of fairness, or equity, in the workplace. This allows an approach to diversity that closely resembles the employee input aspect of quality management programs like ISO 9000."

A *Globe and Mail* story on the instrument reported that the EQ "allows companies to gauge employee attitudes toward policies and their co-workers. Responses are graded along a five-point graph called the equity continuum. Once companies have administered the survey they can judge where they need to concentrate resources."

The objectives of the Equity Quotient survey are to:

- Provide a reliable measurement of equity within the workplace along the equity continuum.

- Provide a means to identify the next steps in a diversity program.

- Provide a means to track the development of equity initiatives.

- Monitor the relationship between equity and performance.

- Provide a supportive process for the implementation of the diversity program.

Through extensive testing of the EQ survey in a number of organizations, an organization can now successfully determine where it sits on the equity continuum. The result is a valid, reliable, and sensitive tool for measuring an organization's level of perceived fairness in employment practices and employee attitudes. In addition, since norms have been developed for the questions used in the EQ survey, an organization can compare its results (answers) to the median. Thus unlike non-normed opinion surveys, the EQ survey is repeatable and can be used to measure the progress of a diversity strategy. In other words, the EQ survey is not a snapshot in time; it actually provides a predictive capacity not available in non-normed instruments. Using the Equity Quotient survey, the organization can consistently and reliably measure progress over time.

Several organizations have used the Equity Quotient survey to find their place on the equity continuum. One that has received substantial public attention is Union Gas, a wholly owned subsidiary of Vancouver's Westcoast Energy Inc. As mentioned earlier, the company is a natural gas storage, transmission, and distribution utility serving approximately 680,000 residential, commercial, and industrial customers in southwestern Ontario.

On May 16, 1995, Union Gas was featured in a story in the *Globe and Mail's* Report on Business Change Page. The article, entitled "Return on Equity," highlighted the utility's experiences with the Equity Quotient. Let us look at how the organization used this instrument to assess its employees' attitudes.

The Union Gas Case

Union Gas sent the Equity Quotient questionnaire to approximately 600 employees—41 percent female, 59 percent male, 10 percent racial minority, and 6 percent employees with disabilities. Employees were told that the major objective of the Equity Quotient questionnaire was to provide a benchmark of employees' perceptions of fairness and to measure progress over time (internally and compared to other companies). Another major objective of Union Gas was to provide a basis to set specific goals and timetables that were not related to representation statistics in order to avoid the perception of quotas.

The Equity Quotient survey measures employees' perceptions along eight major dimensions that are seen as basic to the assessment of fairness. Some of these are similar to dimensions found in regular employee attitude surveys such as management consistency and career development. But you will see that there are other variables that are unique to measurements of fairness.

These are the eight separate variables of the Equity Quotient survey along with the specific areas that are being measured by each dimension.

1. Acceptance of the Business Case: Extent to which the business case is accepted as a "win-win" by all groups.

   - Extent to which the level of productivity or efficiency improves with diversity.

   - Extent to which customer relations improve with diversity.

   - Extent to which community and public support improves.

   - Extent to which hiring and promotion standards improve.

   - Extent to which understanding of what represents good performance improves.

   - Extent to which career-development counselling improves.

   - Extent to which fairness of treatment for all employees improves.

   - Extent to which training and development opportunities improve.

2. Workplace Distance: Extent to which workplace members accept the potential of any group, including white males.

   - Acceptance level of white males.

   - Acceptance level of women.

   - Acceptance level of Chinese, Japanese, and Koreans.

- Acceptance level of Asians and Indo-Pakistanis.

- Acceptance level of people with disabilities.

- Acceptance level of Canadian aboriginal people.

- Acceptance level of black people.

- Acceptance level of gays and lesbians.

3. Systems: Extent to which systems are perceived as being open, fair/equitable, and individualized.

   - Extent to which the company has a fair system for evaluating employee performance.

   - Extent to which employees are informed of job openings.

   - Extent to which applications for job openings are fairly considered.

   - Extent to which promotions and transfers are made fairly.

   - Evaluation of compensation compared to others within the company who have a similar level of responsibility.

4. Standards of Behaviour: Extent to which there is a spirit of mutual respect, collegiality, and due process in place to deal with harassment and discrimination effectively.

   - Extent to which people compliment one another.

   - Extent to which verbal abuse is directed to individual employees.

   - Extent to which flirting with one another is acceptable.

   - Extent to which casual remarks or salutations are demeaning.

   - Extent to which joking about women, racial minorities, or other groups is offensive.

- Extent to which language used is offensive.

- Extent to which demands for sexual acts are a condition for continued employment, favourable work assignments, or other rewards.

- Extent to which people are courteous to one another.

- Extent to which grabbing and touching in inappropriate ways occur.

- Extent to which bulletin board, locker room, or work station displays are offensive.

- Extent to which male employees open doors and carry packages for women.

- Extent to which remarks are inappropriately sexual or racial.

- Extent to which physical and sexual assault occurs.

5. Career Development: Extent to which career opportunities governed by merit/barriers due to stereotypes have been addressed.

  - Extent to which achievements on the job are an advantage.

  - Extent to which seniority in the organization is an advantage.

  - Extent to which having a post-secondary degree or professional qualifications is an advantage.

  - Extent to which supervisor likes you is an advantage.

  - Extent to which willingness to move from location to location is an advantage.

  - Extent to which luck is an advantage.

  - Extent to which race or ethnic affiliations are an advantage.

  - Extent to which family responsibilities are an advantage.

- Extent to which gender is an advantage.

- Extent to which age is an advantage.

- Extent to which getting along with co-workers is an advantage.

- Extent to which physical appearance is an advantage.

- Extent to which willingness to work long hours is an advantage.

- Extent to which a willingness to use leisure time to improve oneself is an advantage.

- Extent to which knowing the right people in the organization is an advantage.

- Extent to which current job position within the organization is an advantage.

- Extent to which family connections within the organization are an advantage.

6. Workplace Flexibility: Extent to which the workplace is aware of employees' accommodation needs and is open to being flexible to address them.

   - Ease of handling family/personal situations during working hours.

   - Convenience of work schedule.

   - Control over scheduling work hours.

   - Extent to which supervisor works with employee to help get the flexibility required on work schedule.

   - Effect of family/personal responsibilities on relationships with co-workers.

   - Effect of family/personal responsibilities on being seen as a committed employee.

- Effect of family/personal responsibilities on getting important work assignments.

- Effect of family/personal responsibilities on being promoted.

- Level of stress due to family/personal life situations.

- Level of stress due to child-care issues.

- Level of stress due to teen issues.

- Level of stress due to elder/dependant-care issues.

- Level of stress due to health/physical fitness.

- Level of stress due to health of family members or people close to you.

- Level of stress due to legal issues.

- Level of stress due to worries about losing job.

- Level of stress due to changes in spouse's or partner's work situation.

- Level of stress due to worries about spouse or partner losing his/her job.

- Level of stress due to work schedule.

- Level of stress due to work load.

- Level of stress due to work-related travel.

- Level of stress due to daily travel time to and from work.

- Level of stress due to conflict between religious practices and work requirements.

- Level of stress due to relationship with spouse or partner.

- Level of stress due to financial/money problems.

- Level of stress due to relationship with other employees.

- Level of stress due to other factors.

7. Work Environment: Extent to which the work environment fosters commitment, provides satisfaction, helps others learn the ropes, and is open to change.

   - Evaluation of organization as a place to work.

   - Evaluation of organization as a place to work compared to earlier.

   - Evaluation of satisfaction with the kind of work.

   - Extent to which work group helps new employees learn the ropes.

   - Extent to which employee would work here again given the opportunity.

8. Management Consistency: Extent to which management does as it says it will and is fair and credible.

   - Extent to which management responds to survey issues.

   - Extent to which supervisor deals fairly with everyone.

   - Extent to which management does as it says it will.

   - Extent to which management is credible.

The types of questions asked in the Equity Quotient survey may appear to be somewhat intrusive. Thus the instrument was pre-tested to determine how respondents would feel about addressing issues not normally found in traditional employee surveys. Union Gas was the first test. The instrument received an impressive 90 percent completely voluntary response rate compared to the usual response rate of 65 to 70 percent.

Let us review how Union Gas did in each category.

- Acceptance of the Business Case: 2 - 2.5

- Workplace Distance: 2 - 2.5

- Systems: 1 - 1.5

- Standards of Behaviour: 2.5 - 3

- Career Development: 2 - 2.5

- Workplace Flexibility: 2.5

- Work Environment: 2.5

- Management Consistency: 2.5

Overall, Union Gas scored between a 2 and a 2.5 on the equity continuum. You will remember that we indicated that we estimate the vast majority of North American companies to be between a 0 and 2. Thus the organization had a good base from which to build the diversity strategy. This is not to say that the EQ survey did not uncover some issues.

As we can see, the company fell down in the area of systems, the extent to which it is perceived to be open, fair, and individualized. Many employees in the organization felt that the promotional system, for example, was based more on "who you know" than merit and ability. Less than 30 percent of employees surveyed—well below the Canadian norm—indicated that promotions were made fairly. Other items that were below the norm and contributed to the company's lower score in the systems area were the perception of fair performance evaluations, job information, and fair consideration of all job applications. The good news was that there did not seem to be a major gender or race bias in the responses. That is, just as many women felt these systems were unfair as men. This indicates that the problem is probably more systemic than attitudinal.

Union Gas also found that some staff were not at ease with gays and lesbians and some said they would not want an Asian or a person with a disability as a direct supervisor. The issue related to gays and lesbians was more evident for males and unionized workers. Lower responses concerning Asian and disabled supervisors occurred for Caucasians than for racial minorities.

Perhaps the most important information gleaned from the EQ survey related to issues of workplace harassment and discrimination. Almost 50 percent of employees did not agree that managers reacted quickly and appropriately after they had been told of offensive behaviour. This appears to affect employees' willingness to tell people in authority about such behaviour. The response encouraged Union Gas to strengthen its existing anti-discrimination/harassment statement and consider further training for supervisors and managers in this area.

Another finding that was confirmed by the survey was the large number of employees who felt that having a university degree was more important than merit in getting ahead. Here again, the organization was not substantially above the norm on this issue. We see "credentialism" in almost every organization across this land. It is only recently that employers are beginning to experience hiring and promoting based solely on degrees as a problem. A cover story in *Canadian Business* magazine in 1995 entitled "Devoured By Degrees" highlighted the credentialism problem. The article stated, "The Canadian dream has always been founded on the possibility of personal mobility—the notion that an individual can seize on new opportunities as they arise. Educational requirements are now tarnishing that dream, locking people into their current jobs and barring new entrants.... The ironclad demand for degrees or diplomas means that the next Bill Gates may be locked out of a profession to which he is ideally suited."

The EQ survey showed Union Gas that its employees felt the company had a problem with credentialism. Based on this feedback, the company has already made changes in recruitment practices. For example, it has shifted some hiring from human resources, who may likely rely on paper qualifications, to line managers, who may be more familiar with the transferable skills required on the job. This has effected another change, which is to train managers in bias-free interviewing techniques.

Union Gas eventually intends to use the EQ survey information as a baseline to test correlation between employee satisfaction and customer satisfaction. This is an upcoming area of research for Dr. Johnson's company. Making such correlations will allow organizations to link improvements in fairness with tangible bottom-line measures. Johnson expects this will provide empirical evidence for the business case, i.e., the more fair an organization is, the greater will be its productivity and competitiveness.

Linking the Qualitative and Quantitative Data

The value of a tool like the Equity Quotient survey is that it was designed to do what it does—measure fairness. One does not need to infer from other surrogate measures. We believe the EQ survey to be unique in this respect and trust that it will become the benchmark qualitative measure of equity in the workplace. We also believe that qualitative measures are the only true way to assess fairness and the value of diversity. But an instrument like the EQ survey can also help an organization interpret quantitative data.

Earlier we stated that unbalanced representation numbers are a signal for the existence of unfairness. The EQ survey result builds on this premise by using representation demographics in the interpretation of results. While not being so finely tuned as to violate anonymity, respondents are asked to identify themselves, anonymously, by sex, minority status, age, and certain other characteristics. This permits a comparison of responses between men and women and whites and people of colour, for example. The analyst can then look for statistically significant differences in responses between various groups. The hypothesis is that, if there are no differences in responses between groups, there are no differences in the perceptions of fairness. In a totally fair employment system (i.e. a Five), all groups, regardless of background, perceive the employment system as fair.

In a diversity program, employee perception is reality and the perception of fairness among the employee population is the best measure of your progress towards a Five. Employees' opinions about the nature and quality of the employment process help us measure the opportunities for improvement.

There is one other approach to estimate the fairness in an employment system and that is to benchmark the organization against others in the industry. This benchmarking will not be based on employee perception but on initiatives pursued in a diversity program. Let us review this model.

ANOTHER APPROACH —
BENCHMARK COMMITMENT SURVEYS

While the Equity Quotient survey answers the question of fairness "compared to what," a benchmark survey looks at fairness "compared to whom." These surveys are usually administered simultaneously in many organizations in a particular industry. Thus they tend to be good predictors of performance-limiting behaviours such as slowdowns, tardiness, absenteeism, turnover, and the potential for third-party organizing activities in one industry.

In August 1994, the American Institute of Certified Public Accountants conducted a diversity-related benchmarking survey focusing on women's status and work/family issues. The survey was sent to more than 5,300 non-sole-practitioner accounting firms through the managing partners. A total of 1,710 questionnaires were completed and returned, a respectable response rate of approximately 32 percent.

The firms were first asked to provide demographic information regarding male and female professional staff. The survey showed that nearly two-thirds of all full-time professional staff in the industry were male while more than seven out of ten part-time positions were female. The study also found that while females represented only one-third of full-time staff, almost 50 percent of full-time professionals leaving the firms were females. Using demographic information, the survey indicated some other "oil lights."

Some of the most startling quantitative information concerned the demographics in the senior positions in accounting firms. Nearly nine out of every ten partners of responding firms were male. Less than one-fourth of the directors employed by firms were females, which was also the case for the next higher position, principals. The survey also showed that some degree of job ghettoization appeared to be occurring in the accounting field. While a vast majority of males were concentrated at the top of the organization, almost half of junior positions, such as staff accountants, were represented by females. What are these oil lights telling us? It is difficult to determine without some specific feedback from employees, but these quantitative data could mean that the work environment is not conducive to women.

This survey also looked at some of the policies surrounding work and family balance. The majority of firms responding to the survey—97 percent—did not offer any alternative work arrangements for partners, a practice that would provide employees with children with more flexible work options. A majority of firms also indicated that they offered only one type of family-related program—maternity leave—and few were planning to extend options regarding work and family in the future.

The AICPA benchmarking survey encouraged many public accounting firms in the industry to review their own quantitative and qualitative information. Within a year, the Canadian Institute of Chartered Accountants sponsored a forum with four of the major national public accounting firms to review their progress in the area of diversity. Among other things, the group discussed both quantitative and qualitative aspects of diversity, such as systemic discrimination in the Canadian accounting profession, using the AICPA study as a benchmark. Shortly thereafter, at least two of the Canadian firms began to increase their emphasis on diversity. In Chapter 5, we highlighted the efforts of one of these progressive firms, Ernst & Young.

A benchmark study can be used as another approach to measuring fairness. Like the other approaches mentioned earlier, it does not rely solely on the quantitative representation data. The benchmark survey uses gathered information as an industry standard against which an organization can compare itself.

In 1995, Omnibus Consulting conducted a unique benchmarking survey of more than 200 major Canadian employers. The survey was designed to determine how many organizations had initiated a diversity strategy. Most of these organizations were in the private sector and employed more than 100 employees. The survey found that more than 70 percent of these organizations had already initiated a diversity program. It also indicated that these organizations would continue to pursue diversity regardless of the existence of employment equity legislation.

This survey was used to generate a group of organizations interested in the field of diversity for business reasons. The Canadian Diversity Network has been launched to help Canadian organizations gather information on key themes of a proper diversity program such as management commitment, employee involvement, awareness and understanding, alignment to business strategy, and proper measurement techniques. At the end of the book you will find an application form so your organization can join this important network.

CONCLUSION

One of the most important lessons to be learned from the history of legislated fairness is that a truly effective diversity program must not rely solely on the numerical representation of a work force to measure the success of a program. When governments encourage organizations to look at representation numbers, they inadvertently distract attention from the real equity issues. Concentrating on the numbers has proven to be an ineffective approach to eliminating discrimination in the workplace. The achievement of numerical targets had little to do with the reduction of discrimination or the achievement of fairness in the employment system.

Fairness in employment systems is really about the perceptions of employees. In this chapter, we have reviewed four ways to measure those perceptions. We recommend you use a normed opinion survey instrument, which will allow an organization to consistently and reliably measure how fair its employment system is compared to Canadian norms. This information is vital to charting the progress of a diversity strategy over a long period of time.

We have also looked at the value of benchmarking studies to measure the fairness of an employment system. Benchmarking studies allow an organization to review its particular diversity strategy compared to others in the industry. Benchmarking can also be an effective way to guide a strategy in the absence of legislative fiat.

In the next chapter, we will look at how to incorporate the qualitative information gathered into an effective diversity strategy. We will review a seven-step approach to achieving a Five—an equitable employment system.

Chapter Nine

THE SEVEN STEPS TO A FIVE

Thus far we have examined the basic components of a successful diversity initiative. These components form the basic building blocks of a strong diversity program and without them, a program will undoubtedly fail. But although they are the basic building blocks, they are not yet a house. In this chapter, we will look at how they fit together to form an effective program.

We will outline a seven-step process that can be used to initiate a diversity strategy within any organization. This process will move an organization along the equity continuum towards the ultimate goal of an equitable employment system. The seven steps are:

1. Needs analysis and preliminary work plan

2. Communications and education

3. Data collection

4. Data analysis

5. Planning

6. Systems change

7. Implementation

We will be highlighting the specific case of Sunnybrook Health Science Centre (SHSC). Although Sunnybrook has not completed all seven steps, it is well on its way to implementing a proper program. In reality, no one organization has completed all seven steps in this long-term evolutionary process. However, we will provide concrete examples for any step yet to be completed by Sunnybrook.

THE CASE OF SUNNYBROOK HEALTH SCIENCE CENTRE

Sunnybrook is a 1,319-bed hospital with acute-care and long-term-care beds. The hospital opened in 1948 for the care of veterans and responded to the need for acute-care civilian beds in the 1960s by becoming the first university teaching complex in Ontario. As a leader in health care in Canada, Sunnybrook depends on the expertise of its staff. The hospital employs about 4,300 people (full and part-time), including almost 1,200 registered nurses. About 300 medical/dental practitioners are affiliated full-time with the hospital.

SHSC prides itself on being a well-managed business in addition to providing excellent patient care. The leaders of the organization recognized early that they needed to go past the limited perspective of legislated employment equity and pursue a more aggressive program. The name of the program reflected this wider perspective. It was called Valuing Diversity. The goal of the Valuing Diversity program was to foster an appreciation and understanding of differences that people brought in to the health-care facility. It was hoped that this would enhance interpersonal relationships among members of diverse groups and ensure equity in the delivery of patient care and in the workplace.

Identifying the Need for a Diversity Program

The demographic shifts in the population were the driving force behind the Valuing Diversity program as the hospital felt the effects of those shifts—their employees and patients were from increasingly diverse backgrounds. In addition, both employees and patients had become less amenable to assimilating into a homogeneous system and were demanding that their differences be acknowledged. This inclination represented a significant departure from the "early days" when the predisposition was to "fit in." In the face of changing employee needs and patient demands, the ability to respond to diversity issues became increasingly important to Sunnybrook.

"We considered developing a valuing diversity program because we needed to do it, not because it was going to be a government directive," explains Tom Closson, President of Sunnybrook. He admits the process that Sunnybrook went through to reach consensus on moving forward with diversity was an arduous one that took more than a year. But hindsight has proven the team was right in taking the time they did before embarking on this important initiative.

In 1992, SHSC began a transformation called Patient Focused Care. This initiative eliminated the traditional professional departments and created clinical teams to manage the care of patients with similar needs. The hospital decentralized staff into multi-functional teams in order to reduce the number of individuals that patients encountered and to empower the staff as part of the care team.

The Patient Focused Care plan looked good on paper, but getting staff to "buy in" was a real challenge. Sunnybrook decided to focus on understanding the people issues that could be barriers to shifting from profession-focused care to patient-focused care. For these reasons, SHSC committed itself to a multi-year Valuing Diversity initiative. The goal of the initiative is to provide the highest-quality patient-focused care possible by removing the visible and invisible barriers to fairness, staff may face in their work environment.

Integration with the Business Strategy

Early in 1994, Sunnybrook developed a framework for Valuing Diversity that was integrated with the new business perspective of patient-focused care. This framework was divided into two major components, one dealing with patients, called Barrier-free Services, the other dealing with employment issues, called Managing Diversity.

The component related to barrier-free services recognized that the planning and delivery of health-care services must take into account the needs of the population the hospital was now serving. It was important to understand how various groups using the hospital perceived and accessed health care in order to ensure the fair or equitable delivery of that care. Ultimately this would lead to an improvement in the quality of service delivery.

The second component of the Valuing Diversity program, called Managing Diversity, was a comprehensive managerial process for developing an environment that works for all employees. The approach included all employees and was not meant as preferential treatment. The SHSC definition of diversity included "any characteristic that helps shape a person's attitudes, behaviours, perspective, and interpretation of what is 'normal' such as race, gender, age, ethno-cultural background, socio-economic status, sexual orientation, religion, education, marital status, family status, etc."

Managing diversity forced managers to take a hard look at the system and ask, "Why doesn't the system work naturally for everyone? What has to be done to allow it to do so? Will the cultural roots of Sunnybrook allow us to take the necessary actions? If not, what root changes do we have to make?"

Managing Diversity was presented to managers as a process, not a program. Managers were not expected to follow a step-by-step procedure but started with managers gaining a conceptual understanding of diversity issues that would then give them the ability to handle diversity issues. Furthermore, it was envisioned that managers would participate in the development of the initiative by soliciting feedback from their own staff.

Sunnybrook's process for the implementation of its diversity strategy used an implementation schedule similar to the chart at the end of the chapter. This chart outlines the seven major steps in the diversity initiative and the key milestones over a three-year period. This type of schedule will allow the organization to determine specific financial requirements by fiscal quarter and to control the major cost elements in the diversity initiative.

Let us review each major step to chart the implementation of an effective plan.

STEP 1: THE NEEDS ANALYSIS AND PRELIMINARY WORK PLAN

The first step of the seven-step program is to conduct a comprehensive needs analysis in preparation for the diversity initiative. This is primarily a research stage that will identify all the elements involved in the initiative and determine the relevant timings and allocation of resources. The step will end with a work plan and chart similar to the one at the end of the chapter. It will also end with an understanding of the financial resources that can realistically be dedicated to the diversity initiative. This identification of costs with the implementation schedule will form the basis of the preliminary work plan.

The major cost elements to be considered before embarking on the diversity initiative are:

• Human Resource Information System (HRIS) capabilities

• The need for education

• Administration of the employment systems review

• Administration of quantitative and qualitative surveys

Much data will be collected in the research undertaken to implement a diversity program. Most of these data will be stored in a Human Resource Information System. Before the diversity plan starts, the manager of information services must evaluate the present HRIS to determine if it can accommodate the future requirements of the process. Attempting to negotiate the cost later in the process will prove difficult.

In particular, the HRIS should be able to track the recruitment, hiring, and promotion of each employee as well as information regarding training attendance. It will also be important that the HRIS be able to break down jobs into national occupational classifications by geographic area in a completely confidential manner. It would be impossible to track this information manually, an up-to-date HRIS system will be a very important tool. The cost of purchasing or updating a new HRIS could be quite high, so it must be integrated early into the planning process.

Education is another major cost element in the diversity strategy. Most organizations budget for some level of education and training every year, but the degree of education required in a properly implemented diversity program could absorb the entire training budget for the fiscal year. Thus it will be important to determine early in the needs analysis stage the level of education required.

The budget for education will depend on how many employees are expected to go through a diversity education session. In an earlier chapter, we discussed the importance of education and communications in a properly designed diversity initiative. Given the hostile environment surrounding diversity issues, many organizations choose to take all employees through some form of awareness education. But the cost of doing this could be prohibitive. Senior and middle management and supervisory staff require more in-depth education because they will be responsible for implementing diversity initiatives in the future, so an organization should at least budget to cover awareness sessions for this group.

We recommend that they have at least one day of diversity education, ideally from an outside source. This will mean budgeting anywhere from $1,000 to $5,000 per day of training, depending on the supplier. The number of days required will obviously depend on the number of employees within the organization. Diversity education sessions are most effective with 35 to 40 participants. The cost of this type of education will be an important investment to ensure the success of the diversity initiative.

There are less costly ways to introduce diversity education. These approaches sometimes involve members of the advisory committee. For example, National Grocers/Loblaws used a consultant to design a train-the-trainer program for members of the advisory committee to deliver. The advisory committee educated hundreds of employees throughout the organization. The committee members also acted as resource guides on the material developed to ensure it met their training needs. This allowed the organization to save on the design costs of an educational program and let employees know that the diversity initiative was customized for the organization. The final product, inclusive of development and delivery costs, was approximately $50 to $100 per employee.

The process used by Sunnybrook has proven to be very democratic. Every employee has attended a diversity educational session, an impressive undertaking and challenge due to the hundreds of staff that work on varying shifts. However, the organization wanted to ensure that the focus on diversity was accepted and made a priority all the way from the executive team to managers, supervisors, and front-line staff.

Other organizations have used external consultants to produce videos and newsletters or organize employee hotlines. These initiatives can be useful but may not be necessary or even appropriate. An organization must ensure that it does not "overcommunicate" the diversity issues to create suspicion in the minds of employees. The necessity of these extras should also be considered as "opportunity costs." That is, the cost of these items should be compared to other essentials in the program. For example, the cost of a 15-minute introductory video can range from $15,000 to $20,000, which could be the price of an entire train-the-trainer program.

The other major costs to be considered in the needs analysis will be the administration of the employment systems review and the surveys. A proper employment systems review can be conducted by members of the advisory committee. Here again, education for these individuals will have to be considered immediately. Advisory committee members will need to be taught how to recognize systemic bias as well as understand relevant human rights legislative concepts such as discrimination, harassment, and accommodation. The major expense, however, will be the opportunity costs for the wages of those who are conducting the review. In our implementation schedule, the employment systems review takes well over one year. Thus it will be important to include the substitute wage cost for members who are active on the committee.

Costs associated with the quantitative and qualitative survey should also be estimated. In Chapter 7, we recommended that the quantitative self-identification survey be combined with the educational sessions. This will save on the need for an administration bureaucracy to be set up. However, the qualitative survey should not be combined with the educational sessions unless it is conducted before the class. This will avoid generating a "halo effect" on the responses. If the survey is done separately, the cost can range from about $25 to $35 per employee and does not include the communication and focus groups. Here again, it is essential that these costs be included in the initial stages of a program.

Once the organization has surveyed the HRIS and determined the budget for the major cost elements of the program, it should seek approval to proceed and move to the next stage, communications and education.

STEP 2: COMMUNICATIONS AND EDUCATION

The implementation schedule leaves approximately six months for the initial communications and education. It is highly likely that further education will be required once the equity issues have been identified in the employment systems review and the qualitative survey. Communications in a well-run program will be ongoing.

We have already covered the necessity of designing an effective communications strategy. It is essential to manage for the possibility of a negative environment that could sabotage a well-thought-out diversity program even before it begins. The strategy must have a logical beginning (launch), a middle (assessment), and end (solutions). Much of the strategy will involve the workings of the advisory committee.

Specific communication components to be considered are

- The terms of reference for the advisory committee

- Requesting nominations to the advisory committee

- The appointment of the advisory committee

- Launching a clear diversity policy statement

- Administration of quantitative and qualitative surveys

- Implementation of the employment systems review

- Feedback of survey results

- Launching new anti-harassment/discrimination policies

- The establishment of goals and timetables

- The establishment of the equity plan

Once a clear policy statement has been established, an effective communications strategy must seek to continually shift the focus away from legislated fairness and concentrate on diversity. It must also reinforce the vision of the Five to all employees.

An important vehicle for communicating the message will be educational sessions for staff. Educational sessions can be used to introduce the vision and identify the attitudinal and systemic barriers that stand in the way of getting to a Five. These barriers are the forms of discrimination previously discussed. Few employees have much experience dealing openly with issues of gender, race, nationality, age, etc. These issues are simply not discussed. Employees realize that they exist but are unwilling to mention them for fear of being politically incorrect or being seen as racist or sexist. A good example is the issue of workplace harassment. In several organizations, we work with many employees who have reported that they faced some form of workplace harassment. Yet few had actually reported it because they were unaware of the procedure established by the organization. They were also unsure if what they were facing was actually harassment according to the law or corporate policy. The educational program can serve to clarify this situation and give the organization an opportunity to announce or reinforce an anti-harassment policy.

At Sunnybrook, initial Valuing Diversity education sessions were completed in early April 1994. Hospital-wide communications began shortly thereafter with articles and brochures included with pay statements. Both the education and communications initiatives were to develop sensitivity and awareness of diversity issues, not to announce a plethora of set programs. The theme stressed evolutionary rather than revolutionary change. This stage was meant to foster an appreciation and understanding of differences that people bring to the workplace—in particular the differences of patients, residents, and families that could create barriers in accessing hospital services.

Tom Closson, who has become the champion for diversity, asks, "How can we be expected to provide patient-focused care if we are not conscious of the differences of our patients that come to our hospital? Secondly, how can we expect our staff to be patient-focused if they are not understanding and focused on each other's needs?"

Once an organization has effectively created an appropriate environment for the diversity program by way of education, it is ready to move to stage three—data gathering.

STEP 3: QUANTITATIVE AND QUALITATIVE DATA GATHERING

Any major organization change has to be measured. In order for it to be measured, data must be gathered. If you are attempting to create a more equitable employment system—the goal of a diversity initiative—the question must be asked, "How will you know when you get there?"

The government's legislated fairness approach would suggest that you have achieved an equitable system when there is change in the representation statistics in the workplace. Thus a legislated fairness initiative will encourage organizations to focus on the gathering of quantitative data. In 1990, the Conference Board of Canada reported that, on average, federally regulated organizations allocated over 70 percent of their employment equity budgets to the collection and administration of quantitative, representation data. The focus on the numbers clearly channelled human and financial resources away from the development and implementation of equity itself.

Organizations committed to diversity may collect quantitative data but will focus their programs on the collection of qualitative data. The answer to the question of knowing how fair an employment system is will not be based on the representation of groups. It will be based on what employees tell you.

Sunnybrook conducted its quantitative survey, not because of legislation, but in order to get a clear idea of the demographic make-up of its organization. This allowed Sunnybrook to understand how closely the hospital staff reflected the patient base. These data would also be used for the gap analysis in the next stage.

Sunnybrook then conducted an attitude survey to determine

qualitative diversity issues. This survey was followed by a process of conducting focus groups to flush out the key issues. The organization knew that a valid qualitative survey should be filled out by all members of the work force so in order to ensure a good response rate, a separate communication strategy was used to launch the opinion survey.

In Chapter 8 we wrote about the need to measure in a consistent and predictable manner the perception of equity in the employment system compared to Canadian norms. We introduced the Equity Quotient, a new instrument on the market designed to do this. Sunnybrook used the Equity Quotient Survey to determine how equitable its employment system was compared to the rest of industry. They also used the EQ survey to compare the perception of equity among various groups. This allowed Sunnybrook to concentrate on the real equity issues such as discrimination and harassment and move past representation numbers as a sole means of measurement.

Representation statistics can, in some cases, indicate the absence of equity but they can never demonstrate its presence. We have encountered some striking examples of what anyone would see as inequity in organizations that have very high representation statistics. For example, we were called into one government office that was highly diverse in culture and race. Yet upon closer examination, not one employee felt the office employment system was fair. In the area of career development, almost 50 percent of employees reported that there were limitations to career development and that striving for excellence was not worthwhile. Since the survey data were broken down by gender, age, and race, it was easy to determine that barriers to career development was a more prevalent issue among women and non-white employees. It was clear that in this department the numerical representation of various groups was not enough to ensure fair treatment of employees.

The qualitative data collected from a properly designed attitude survey will need to be coupled with the information gathered in the employment systems review. Earlier we stated that the ESR is used primarily to collect information regarding systemic discrimination. Some of this systemic discrimination occurs because informal procedures that are commonly used in the system cause inequity. For example, an organization had a summer employment program that was informally reserved for the sons and daughters of employees. The diversity advisory committee thought this practice could discriminate against more qualified candidates who may have no connections to the organization. Their suspicions were confirmed by the employee opinion survey, which showed that most employees felt "who you know" was the major inequity in their system.

The implementation schedule shows that the employment systems review can take twice as long as the implementation of an attitude survey. This is because of the numerous people and subcommittees that can be involved in this process. It will be important to continually compare the feedback from the ESR with the more detailed attitude survey. If both instruments have been designed properly, there will be a strong correlation in the information gathered.

The qualitative information will also add relevance to some of the quantitative data. For example, we worked for one organization that sent out a self-identification questionnaire that found the number of women was significantly lower at a very specific part of the career ladder. The quantitative data had shown that the turnover rate for women increased almost 30 percent between the manager and senior manager level. It seemed that a glass ceiling was present but it was difficult to determine from the quantitative information alone. The organization compared the quantitative information to the feedback from the attitude survey. They found that one-quarter of the employees above manager level felt that work and lifestyle options were not acceptable in their work unit even though the company had a very strong public position on the issue. In this case, the survey showed that the problem was clearly more prevalent among female employees. By comparing the quantitative and qualitative data, the organization managed to show that the work and lifestyle issues were the reason behind the lack of retention of women at senior positions.

The collection of quantitative and qualitative data need not be a difficult process. Organizations can integrate this step into education or even regularly scheduled meetings. Once the information has been collected, it will need to be analyzed.

STEP 4: DATA ANALYSIS

The next step in the process is to analyze the quantitative and qualitative data collected. The major objective of this analysis is to determine how fair the employment system is compared to an external measure. There are three external standards to measure data against: availability data, normative data, and best practices.

Quantitative data are analyzed in a process called the gap analysis. It is called "gap" because it compares the gap between the representation data collected in the self-identification survey and the available external work force identified by occupational code. It is important that national occupational codes are used in this analysis rather than the percentage of a particular group in the population as a whole.

The National Occupational Classification (NOC) process classifies every job and assigns it a four-digit identification number. These codes were derived from the national census, which asked respondents to write in the kind of work they were doing and their most important activities or duties. NOC codes are broken down into 11 major categories. They are:

1. Senior managers

2. Middle and other managers

3. Professionals (Skill level A)

4. Semi-professionals and technicians (Skill level B)

5. Supervisors-clerical, sales, and service

6. Supervisors- Manufacturing, Processing, Trades, and Primary Industry

7. Administrative and Senior Clerical

8. Sales and Service (Skill levels A, B, C, D)

9. Skilled crafts and trades

10. Clerical workers

11. Semi-skilled manual workers (Skill Levels A, B, C, D)

This information is then categorized by census metropolitan area (CMA). A CMA is defined as an urban area having a population of at least 100,000 based on the previous census. Once an area becomes a CMA, it is considered separately for economic and social analysis. Statistics Canada has defined 25 CMAs. They are

Calgary, Alberta;	Saskatoon, Saskatchewan;
Chicoutimi-Jonquière, Quebec;	Sherbrooke, Quebec;
Edmonton, Alberta;	St. Catharines, Ontario;
Halifax, Nova Scotia;	St. John's, Newfoundland;
Hamilton, Ontario;	Sudbury, Ontario;
Kitchener,Ontario;	Thunder Bay, Ontario;
London, Ontario;	Toronto, Ontario;
Montreal,Quebec;	Trois-Rivières, Quebec;
Oshawa, Ontario;	Vancouver, British Columbia;
Ottawa-Hull, Ontario;	Victoria, British Columbia;
Quebec City, Quebec;	Windsor, Ontario;
Regina, Saskatchewan;	Winnipeg, Manitoba.
Saint John, New Brunswick;	

Additional information regarding NOC/CMA categories can be obtained though the Data Development and Systems Analysis Directorate, Human Resources Development Canada, Government of Canada.

The analysis of quantitative data is meant only to signal the degree of inequity that may exist in an employment system. That is, it is the oil light. It may signal how well an employment system is reaching talent in the surrounding CMA. Let's say, for example, that the organization is interested in hiring chemists/ engineers. The occupational code for this group is 2112. The self-identification survey will allow employees to identify their job category by group status. If the organization finds the percentage of women in their organization reporting the 2112 code is substantially lower than what is available in the surrounding CMA, this could be an oil light indicating that some form of systemic or attitudinal inequity may exist in the system. If representation numbers are the oil light, the gap analysis could well be thought of as the oil stick.

The quantitative information gathered from the GAP analysis will not be enough to determine the equity of a system. An organization needs to look at two other forms of analysis that use qualitative data. The first is the normative analysis. This analysis allows an organization to identify where it is situated on the equity continuum compared to other organizations. For example, according to the federal government, approximately 24 percent of Canadian women report being sexually harassed in the workplace. If your attitude survey shows that more women than the "norm" (i.e., 24 percent) are being harassed, you probably have a problem with equity. The Equity Quotient Survey, introduced in the last chapter, allows an organization to compare itself to several important normative themes. Without norms, an attitude survey will give only a "snapshot" analysis of an organization's equity situation.

The measurement of the qualitative elements of an employment system shifts the focus of an equity program away from representation numbers to the perception of equity within the organization among various groups. A normative analysis provides an objective benchmark of fairness and a reliable measure of how quickly the organization is moving along the equity continuum. In order to trace this movement, the opinion survey must not be a one-time event. Any proper diversity program will include a schedule of at least three attitude surveys over a ten-year period to determine movement along the continuum.

A normed attitude survey will answer the question "How fair are we compared to what?" Another question to ask is "How fair are we compared to whom?" This can be determined by comparing the organization to best practices in the industry. Earlier we wrote about the Canadian Diversity Network, which is a group of organizations benchmarking on the key areas of an effective diversity initiative. By benchmarking against best practices, an organization can ensure that it is up-to-date on the most innovative initiatives in the field.

A common mistake made in benchmarking against best practices is to assume that all initiatives are transferable between organizations. An employment system is a complex, dynamic entity and change initiatives must be designed to fit the particular corporate culture. Simply copying an equity initiative from another organization may not work effectively because the organization could have a substantially different hierarchy. Best practices may only be "best" for the organization they were designed for. Nevertheless, benchmarking against best practices may be a valuable source for ideas for your own program as long as you use it with other qualitative and quantitative data. In the next chapter, we will outline some best practices in the key areas of a diversity program.

Not only has Sunnybrook joined the Canadian Diversity Network in order to be a benchmark, its president, Tom Closson, has become a member of the Canadian Diversity Advisory Council. This is a group of high-powered Canadian executives representing leading organizations that are committed to the business case for equity. Closson and these other executives provide an effective think tank for analyzing the development of Canadian norms in equity. Information about the work of the CDAC is available through the Canadian Diversity Network (see contact sheet at end of book).

STEP 5: PLANNING

Once an organization has analyzed its position, it begins the task of setting realistic goals and timetables. This stage asks the question "What do we want to achieve by when?" Setting realistic quantitative and qualitative goals is an essential part of the diversity process. The most important goals will be the qualitative ones but a lot of attention has been focused on quantitative goals because of legislative fairness programs.

Many people confuse quantitative goals and timetables with quotas. A quota is an externally set inflexible number set by a government. If this number is not met, some punitive consequence usually results, such as a fine. A goal is a flexible, internally set number that is used to guide progress in a diversity program. Unlike a quota, there is usually not a punitive consequence for missing a goal. While goals and timetables are common to Canadian diversity programs, quotas are not. In fact, there is only one recorded case of government-imposed quotas in Canada. This was the case of Canadian National, which was ordered to hire a specific number of women for non-traditional jobs in the early eighties.

It would appear that quotas and the reliance on representation numbers to guide equity programs have been less than effective in the United States. After more than 30 years of numbers-focused affirmative action programs in the United States, there has been only marginal change in the representation of women and racial minorities in senior positions. As late as 1990, a UCLA study of *Fortune 500* industrial corporations in the United States found that women and racial minorities held less than 5 percent of senior positions. The same study showed that there had been only a 2 percent increase in minorities and women in top executive positions in the previous ten years.

History has shown us that a concentration exclusively on numbers will lead to neither a sustainable change in representation statistics nor a more equitable employment system. Quantitative goals for representation numbers can serve as a means to an end but they must not be the focus of the planning stage. The focus of the planning stage should be the qualitative data gathered from the attitude survey.

The qualitative information analyzed in the normative process will allow an organization to set its priorities. Reducing the gap between the result and the norm on a particular item should become the focus of the diversity strategy once the information has been collected. You will notice in the implementation schedule that this requires a step to obtain approval to proceed. The formulation of realistic qualitative goals should be endorsed by the senior executive group who will be ultimately responsible for their achievement. Once this approval has been obtained, the organization can move to the next step, which is determining how it will achieve the goals and timetables.

This is the stage Sunnybrook sits at today. In order for it to complete the process effectively, it will require a series of meetings with key opinion leaders in the organization to negotiate reasonable goals and timetables. These meetings will also develop ownership for the goals set, an essential consideration of an effective program. If managers and other opinion leaders do not take ownership for a goal, it is highly unlikely to be achieved.

STEP 6: SYSTEM CHANGE

Once an organization has conducted the quantitative and qualitative analysis, completed the employment systems review, and set goals and timetables, it is ready to prepare an equity plan.

This plan is not to be confused with the diversity strategy, which is the entire seven-step process. The equity plan will outline how the specific goal outlined in Step 5 will be achieved over a relatively short term—three to five years. It will also identify the individuals within the organization who will be responsible for implementing the change initiatives.

It may be necessary for an organization to prepare more than one plan because it has several locations, each of which may operate as a separate entity and thus require a completely different strategy than other parts of the organization. Together all the sub-plans in an organization should cover all employees.

A valid equity plan should include the following components:

- A list of policies and practices identified as systemic barriers that will be eliminated during the term of the plan.

- A list of policies and practices identified as systemic barriers that will be eliminated during the term of subsequent plans.

- A list of types of discrimination identified as attitudinal barriers that will be eliminated during the term of the plan.

- A list of types of discrimination identified as attitudinal barriers that will be eliminated during the term of subsequent plans.

- A description of the measures that will be implemented during the term of the plan such as changes to the recruitment, hiring, retention, and promotion systems or innovative accommodation measures.

- A list of numerical goals for the qualitative data that will be achieved during the term of the plan and a description of how the goals were set. It may be helpful to include the normative data the goal was based on to ensure a complete understanding of the goal's relevance.

- A list of numerical goals for quantitative representation data that will be achieved during the term of the plan and a description of how the goals were set. Representation goals will be based on the proportion of job openings in each occupational group. Separate representation goals can be stated for each geographical area covered by the plan.

- A description of the timetable for implementing the measures and achieving the quantitative and qualitative goals.

- A description of how the implementation of the measures and the achievement of the quantitative and qualitative goals will be monitored.

- A description of the measures that have already been implemented.

- A description of the procedure that a person may use to obtain accommodation and the procedure to be used by the organization in responding to a request.

- A summary of employees' comments received during the data gathering and employment systems review process.

- A description of how the organization intends to address concerns raised that have not been covered elsewhere in the equity plan.

Most equity plans use a three-year cycle. This will give the organization enough time to implement and determine major changes to the employment system. However, this period is not so long that the plan becomes irrelevant due to unforeseen changes in the external environment. The plan must be reviewed at least annually to determine ongoing progress.

Any equity plan must include some provision to deal with workplace harassment and discrimination. This begins by developing an anti-harassment/discrimination policy. Most organizations have had some form of harassment policy for many years but have not communicated it to staff because of an unrealistic fear that communicating it could prompt employees to lay complaints that they would not have normally brought forth.

Any organization introducing a valid equity plan must take a more proactive approach to the creation of a harassment/discrimination-free environment. This will mean putting in place a strategy to communicate the policies followed by education throughout the organization. Specialized training for managers regarding the investigation and discipline procedure may also be required.

Sunnybrook has yet to develop its first equity plan. Yet Tom Closson has already indicated that the equity plan will be based on the results of the quantitative, qualitative, and employment systems review. The Sunnybrook equity plan will also be realistic and dates will be established for its accomplishment. In order for the plan to be truly effective, Sunnybrook will need to assure that it assigns accountability for executing the plan. Individual senior managers, including members of the board should be assigned a particular responsibility in the plan and held accountable for implementation. Without such an assignment, it is unlikely that the initiatives will be accomplished. Finally, the plan must have objective criteria to test for success. Sunnybrook may consider using these criteria as means of performance measurement for their managers and supervisors. Since the criteria will be based on valid quantitative and qualitative data, they can easily be tracked and linked to the annual performance evaluation process.

STEP 7: IMPLEMENTATION

One of the biggest shortcomings of legislated fairness programs was that they did not require organizations to implement any plan. The legislation usually contained some vague directive such as "the employer will use best efforts to implement a plan." Since the legislation never defined "best efforts," there was little requirement for progress once a plan had been filed.

A proper diversity program begins after the equity plan has been completed. It starts with the implementation of the equity plan and continues with an ongoing analysis of the execution of key components of the plan. The equity advisory committee will have to closely monitor the implementation of the equity plan and make adjustments to areas where it is not working.

We would recommend that the equity advisory committee prepare a report to the executive within six months of the plan being implemented. This report should include information on quantitative and qualitative progress in the organization such as the number of completed and uncompleted survey returns, number of harassment complaints filed, and changes to employment representation numbers.

The advisory committee should pay particular attention to the following areas:

- The effectiveness of new measures introduced to determine if they are achieving the planned result.

- Changes in organizational strategy, structure, or process that could affect key components of the plan in the short and long term.

- Changes in the work force profile and turnover that may have been caused by the equity plan.

- Changes in leadership, management, business strategy, and vision that may affect the implementation of the equity plan.

- Changes in financial and human resources that could affect the achievability of results.

The equity committee must determine proper implementation by monitoring both inputs and outputs. The most obvious output may be a change in the composition of the work force. It is important to remember that representational numbers can be a signal that some change has taken place in the employment system. If the composition of candidates, new hires, and promotions has changed substantially after an equity plan has been introduced, it may be an indication that something in the plan is working.

The other outputs to be measured will be the qualitative improvements to the employment system. Once an organization has established the key areas of inequity as identified by employees, it can begin to watch these areas closely for improvements. For example, one organization we surveyed found almost 35 percent of employees surveyed indicated that they had been subjected to workplace harassment over the past two years. It was clear from the write-in comments on the survey that most of the harassment was not sexual but based on race or culture.

Some employees said, "I often hear racist comments made at a high level," "A certain degree of harassment [not sexual] is prevalent," "There must be penalties for any insulting or discriminating remarks made by a white person." The survey also indicated that there was less-than-universal tolerance for racial minorities in the organization, indicated by comments such as "On a national level I feel that immigration into Canada has got out of control" and "I am forced to work with people who have a rudimentary knowledge of the English language."

The organization decided to introduce a new workplace harassment/discrimination policy and complaint procedure. This was followed by mandatory training for all staff. Managers were given resource kits and more in-depth training on how to receive and investigate harassment complaints. The organization also began to monitor and track the number of complaints filed every month. These numbers were compiled by the equity committee and reported to the senior board. In this way, the organization could determine if its new emphasis on mutual respect was being taken seriously in the workplace. The organization found that after an initial increase in harassment complaints shortly after the new policy was introduced, complaints decreased by more than 80 percent in less than a year. More importantly, the legal costs of fighting complaints with the human rights commission also declined substantially. The equity committee could actually put a dollar figure on how much this equity initiative had saved the organization.

An organization can also measure inputs to determine effective implementation. An input would be any effort the organization intends to change to effect a certain output. For example, an organization found that "who you know" recruitment was widely considered an inequity in the employment system. The equity committee recommended that every job receive an internal posting and be advertised in at least three external publications in order to maximize outreach. It was relatively easy for the equity committee to track if this practice was being followed by simply monitoring jobs as they were posted.

In Sunnybrook, as in any organization, the implementation of the equity plan will be ensured by careful monitoring and evaluation by the executive and the equity advisory committee.

This will ensure that the organization eventually achieves an equitable employment system based solely on merit and fairness. Since this is an ongoing evolutionary goal, Tom Closson realizes it will not be achieved over the course of one, two, or even several equity plans. The achievement of a Five requires continuous maintenance over the long term. It is something like brushing your teeth—it never really is over.

CRITERIA FOR SUCCESSFUL IMPLEMENTATION

Proper implementation of the employment equity plan will occur if the plan is accountable, measurable, workable, and most importantly integrated with the vision of getting to a Five. These four elements will not guarantee the success of the employment equity plan but it is clear that their absence will guarantee that the plan will fail. Let us begin with the last criterion—integration with the vision.

Integration With the Vision

We like to remind our clients before they begin a diversity program that this will be the largest organizational change the company may ever face. It will confront traditional practices and procedures in the organization and may well seek to change the corporate culture itself. It is important that any recommended change be seen in the context of the overall vision of getting to a Five. If this integration is not done, an organization may exacerbate resistance to the program.

For example, we worked with an organization that had set the goal of getting to a Five. It went through the seven-step process and was finally ready to begin implementation of the plan. It started with the items of fairness that could immediately be affected. The first initiative appeared to be relatively innocuous. The equity advisory committee recommended that the organization rescind its membership in a golf club that had a discriminatory clause in its bylaw. This clause prevented the membership of women and racial minorities. The committee argued that supporting such an organization would be inconsistent with the company's espoused principles of fairness.

The reaction to the recommendation was immediate and fierce. Members of the executive were outraged about the recommendation and felt the committee had gone past its mandate. "We have had a 30-year history with this club!" they argued. "And equity has nothing to do with playing golf."

The battle lines were drawn, with the equity committee members threatening to quit if their recommendation was not accepted and some outspoken members of the executive threatening to disband the committee. The president of the organization eventually resolved the issue by agreeing with the committee and withdrawing support from the golf club. He argued that if the organization was committed to the vision of a Five, all of their actions must be consistent. This action may have been more symbolic than others in the plan, but it was just as important. In fact, it turned out that the action became more than symbolic. Shortly after the organization quit the golf club, the club changed the bylaw, which had been on the books for almost 100 years.

The moral of the story is that every initiative in the equity plan must be seen in the context of the vision. When an equity plan is implemented properly, the vision gives the context for every recommended organizational change. Without this context, any initiative may appear illogical or, in the worst case, unnecessary. When this happens, the initiative is not supported and ultimately not implemented. This leads us to the next criteria of successful implementation—accountability.

Accountability

Any equity plan will be implemented if key leaders in the organization are made accountable for it. This means that components of the plan show up in their business strategy and have been budgeted for. This also means that the performance evaluation and compensation of these leaders will be affected by the successful implementation of the plan.

One of the most common mistakes made by organizations is leaving the accountability of the plan to the employment equity co-ordinator. There is no one individual in an organization who has the power and resources to implement the entire equity plan, the plan to move the organization to a Five. No individual can do it alone.

The first step to achieve accountability for the plan is to get buy-in for the vision. If the key implementers of the plan have not bought in to the vision, there will not be serious movement on the plan.

Buy-in is achieved by effectively communicating the vision to those who will be responsible for implementation. This communication must come from someone who is perceived as a credible leader in the organization, ideally the CEO or president. As the old saying goes, "What interests my boss fascinates the hell out of me." This leader must be able to link the vision of the equity plan to a long-standing value in the organization.

For example, IBM has a long-standing principle of respect for the individual. The vision of an employment system that operates based solely on merit and fairness where no forms of discrimination exist clearly supports this principle. Employees must see that the equity initiative is a continuation of the company's approach to human resources. If this is done, employees are less likely to perceive the equity program as another "flavour of the week."

Once buy-in for the vision has been achieved, key opinion leaders must be shown the strategy to achieve it—the seven steps that have been outlined in this chapter. Leaders must understand how these seven steps will be implemented and the timeframe for each. This will give them a context for their actions and include them in the co-ordinated strategy to achieve a Five.

Out of the strategy come the overall goals of the equity plan. The goals lay out the more immediate steps to be taken to move the organization along the equity continuum. If, for example, an organization is at a 2.5 on the equity continuum, what is the goal for the year 2000? If the overall goal is a 3.5, what are the specific forms of inequity that will need to be reduced in order to achieve it? What are the goals that should be set in these areas?

In order to ensure implementation of an equity plan, it is important to include those who will be required to obtain the goals in the goal-setting process. Goals must be seen as achievable within the given timeframe. The best people to tell you if goals are achievable are the ones who will be accountable for achieving them. This is especially true if the achievement of the goal is connected to the annual performance evaluation process and bonus.

Once realistic goals are set, how to achieve them is laid out in the equity plan. Once again, it is important to include the individuals who will be responsible for achieving the goals in this discussion. It is unlikely that many of the goals in an equity program can be achieved without some increase in resources, either financial or human. Thus questions about who will work on new initiatives or how they will be paid for must be considered by the person responsible for reaching the goal. This person can then establish if there is a need for further resource support or if the goal needs to be adjusted.

Measurable

Another major criterion of proper implementation is measurability of the equity plan. Organizations measure those things that are important to them—budget projections, market share, etc. Measurability is used to determine if a plan is working and how far an organization is from an established goal.

The key element of a proper diversity strategy is that success is measured qualitatively as well as quantitatively. As we have said, equity in the workplace must be about the perception of equity, not just the representation of various groups. Thus the proper measurement of a successful equity initiative will be an instrument that measures the opinion and attitudes of the employees. The representation data, which is the usual focus of an equity plan, can be used as a tool to support this measurement of equity but it cannot be used as a replacement.

In order for measurement of the qualitative elements of equity to be meaningful, they must be compared against an external benchmark. This is where the use of normative data comes in. Normative data give an organization a perspective on how equitable the employment system is compared to others in its industry or in industry in general. Without the normative benchmark, organizations are simply provided with a snapshot of themselves at a given time. The snapshot alone can give an idea of key issues but it cannot provide a comparison of how fair an organization is relative to the rest of the country.

Another reason for using normative data is to track the progress of an organization. If, for example, an organization has a 50 percent turnover in staff from one attitude survey to the other, the population answering the first survey will be considerably different than the one answering the second. A shift in attitude may have nothing to do with the change in the employment system, but it may be because of the different perception of the new work force. It is impossible to say what accounts for the change.

If, however, an organization measures itself against national normative data, it makes little difference if the staff is the same. What is being measured is the gap between the perception of employees and the norm. Thus an organization is attempting to reduce the gap between current perception and the norm of the day.

The same logic can be used for the analysis of representation statistics. The quantitative data from the representation statistics must be presented to the individuals responsible for the implementation of the equity plan. Once again, this quantitative data should be used only as a signal, not as the focus. They are only the oil light.

For example, one of our clients did most of its recruitment for computer science graduates from the universities of Waterloo and Western. For more than ten years, more than 60 percent of computer science graduates from both institutions have been visible minorities. This organization had hired almost 100 computer science graduates over the previous five years and only one had been a visible minority. Now the oil light went off. Either none of the 60 percent of visible minority graduates were the best candidates or there was some form of bias in the recruitment process.

When the recruitment staff looked at the statistics, they accounted for the discrepancy immediately. They had developed a habit of interviewing only those candidates who had attained good marks and also played team sports. There was no real logic behind it, other than the city where the organization was located was very sports-oriented. Either way, this created a systemic inequity for the best candidates who did not play sports. To correct the situation, the recruiters decided to end the practice. They also set a goal of hiring five visible minority graduates to determine if anything had changed. The assumption is that a change in numerical representation signifies a change in the system.

Workable/Achievable

The most frequent question we get in diversity training programs is "Is it possible to get to a Five?" The answer is "We don't know but it is possible to set the vision to get to the Five and take consistent action towards that vision." As long as the vision is not achieved, it becomes a stimulus for the organization to take consistent action.

A good example of this would be President Kennedy in the 1960s. He set a ten-year vision of putting a man on the moon and returning him safely to earth. When he made the statement in 1961, many people thought the objective was impossible. In fact, the most optimistic scientific assessment of the moon mission's chances for success in that year was 50-50. Nonetheless, enough people in Congress were inspired by the Kennedy vision to commit billions of dollars to the project, and they made it happen. But they did not make it happen in Kennedy's lifetime. In fact, the vision became so entrenched that it took on a life of its own and lived past Kennedy.

The vision of a Five must operate the same way. It must be seen as achievable but such a stretch that it will not occur without significant organizational change. This change begins with a realistic assessment of where the organization is and ends with the implementation of a plan that sets out the steps for the change.

The equity plan is not designed to get an organization to a Five overnight—it is an evolutionary change. The plan is designed to take the organization to the next established point on the equity continuum. People responsible for the implementation of the plan will be able to measure their success quantitatively and qualitatively and determine their progress year by year.

Most equity plans will use three- to five-year timelines, but it is unlikely that any organization will achieve its vision in that short a period of time. Thus the vision will not change over the duration of several plans. The vision is simply the long-range ideal to shoot for. A comparable example would be total quality. An organization probably never achieves total quality. It sets the vision of total quality and then takes action to attempt to achieve it.

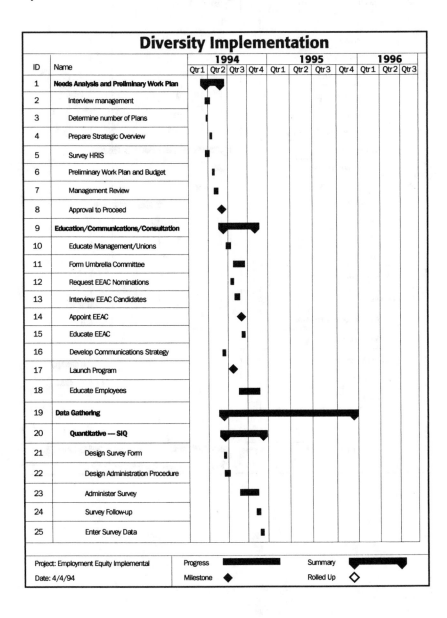

Diversity Implementation

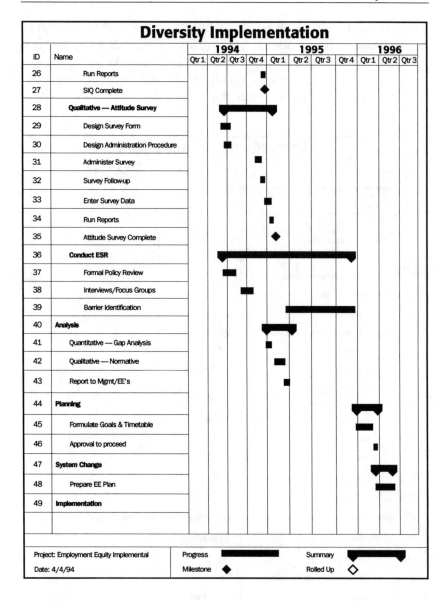

ID	Name	1994				1995				1996		
		Qtr 1	Qtr 2	Qtr 3	Qtr 4	Qtr 1	Qtr 2	Qtr 3	Qtr 4	Qtr 1	Qtr 2	Qtr 3
26	Run Reports				■							
27	SIQ Complete				◆							
28	**Qualitative — Attitude Survey**		▬▬▬▬									
29	Design Survey Form		■									
30	Design Administration Procedure		■									
31	Administer Survey				■							
32	Survey Follow-up				■							
33	Enter Survey Data				■							
34	Run Reports					■						
35	Attitude Survey Complete					◆						
36	**Conduct ESR**		▬▬▬▬▬▬▬▬▬▬▬									
37	Formal Policy Review		■									
38	Interviews/Focus Groups			■								
39	Barrier Identification					▬▬▬▬						
40	**Analysis**					▬▬▬						
41	Quantitative — Gap Analysis					■						
42	Qualitative — Normative					■						
43	Report to Mgmt/EE's					■						
44	**Planning**									▬▬		
45	Formulate Goals & Timetable									▬▬		
46	Approval to proceed									■		
47	**System Change**									▬▬		
48	Prepare EE Plan									▬▬		
49	**Implementation**											

Project: Employment Equity Implemental	Progress	▬▬▬▬	Summary	▬▬▬▬
Date: 4/4/94	Milestone ◆		Rolled Up ◇	

Chapter Ten

THE FAIREST IN THE LAND:
BEST PRACTICES FROM DIVERSITY LEADERS

The research conducted for this book has led us to some highly equitable employment systems. These organizations may not yet have achieved the vision of a Five but they are clearly well on their way. These are also organizations that have incorporated the five key components of an effective diversity strategy.

The fairest in the land (in alphabetical order) are:

1. Aetna Canada

2. Bayer Rubber

3. Canadian Imperial Bank of Commerce

4. Canadian Tire Acceptance Ltd.

5. CASCO Inc.

6. Celestica

7. Connaught Laboratories Limited

8. Consumers Gas

9. Dow Chemical Canada Inc.

10. Ernst & Young

11. General Motors of Canada Limited

12. IBM Canada Ltd.

13. Kmart Canada Limited

14. Kimberly-Clark Inc.

15. London Life Insurance Co.

16. Manulife Financial

17. National Grocers/Loblaws

18. North American Life Assurance Company

19. Seagrams

20. Steelcase Canada Ltd.

21. Sunnybrook Hospital

22. Union Gas

23. Wellington Insurance Company

Is there a common link between the fairest employment systems? Is there something they are doing exceptionally well? We think so and have narrowed it down to four things:

1. Accommodation

2. Diverse work teams

3. Equitable opportunity

4. Dignity and respect

Let us review each characteristic and identify how it shows up in the fairest employment systems.

ACCOMMODATION

When governments talk about the concept of accommodation, they are usually referring to capital changes to a building for wheelchair access. Leaders in the diversity field know that accommodation will include a variety of means to ensure that employees can work effectively and productively in today's workplace. Thus accommodation is any flexibility in practice and procedure without which an employee could not participate actively and effectively in the work force. Common examples of accommodation in the organizations listed above include flexible hours, flex space, job sharing, tele-commuting, recognition of religious difference, and the provision of personal days.

Accommodation is a key characteristic of a successful diversity strategy. In Chapter 1, we wrote about the need to shift to a different human resource management strategy, the need to have managers move out of the Age of Equality, where people are treated the same, to the Age of Equity, where people are treated fairly. In order to do this a manager must begin to acknowledge the different needs of employees (the definition of diversity) rather than ignoring differences. Once a manager has acknowledged a different need, she or he can ensure fair treatment by accommodating that need. In other words, the difference between an organization that stands in the Age of Equality and the Age of Equity is that in the latter the diverse needs of employees are being accommodated.

The Ernst & Young Alternative Work Arrangement Policy

An excellent example of best practice accommodation is the Ernst & Young Alternative Work Arrangement Policy. This progressive accommodation policy is aligned with the firm's strategic plan Mission Millennium. The AWA policy was designed to enhance the organization's stated objective of retaining high-quality people by creating an attractive work environment. It was also seen as a way for the organization to optimize their most important resource–their people.

Ernst & Young is well aware of the business realities surrounding accommodation issues. They know that competition for qualified professional staff will be increasing over the next few years. For example, the number of CAs in public practice is projected to decline by the year 2015 from 40 percent to 30 percent of total CAs. Thus E&Y, like other professional firms, can no longer afford to lose the best people simply because they have not responded to employee needs.

The Canadian Institute of Chartered Accountants has identified child care and family responsibilities and the need to balance career and lifestyle as key diversity issues for the entire profession. Ernst & Young has responded to these issues by introducing a progressive Alternative Work Arrangement (AWA) policy. Ernst & Young defines an AWA as "any work arrangement which is different than the traditional work arrangement practiced amongst the office and staff level. For example, different hours, different physical location, specific needs related to work related travel, educational pursuits, childcare/eldercare, etc. An AWA may include part-time work, job sharing, a compressed work week, etc."

Many organizations, including other major professional firms, have introduced Alternative Work Arrangement policies. What distinguishes the Ernst & Young AWA from the rest is the acknowledgment that employees are encouraged to use the AWA opportunities where possible. In most organizations, AWAs are not used because employees feel using them could be damaging to their careers. They fear that they could be labelled as uncommitted or less productive because they are working outside of the "norm." Thus many AWA policies sit on the books, looking good but with little effectiveness because they are not used.

Ernst & Young recognized this dilemma and has designed a strategy to overcome it. The AWA policy and procedure were introduced as part of a full-day training program for all management. Members of the diversity team provided participants with an overview of the policy and its implications for the firm and dealt with questions of implementation. The discussions in these educational sessions dealt directly with the typical perceptions of an AWA being seen as a career-limiting move. The leaders of the firm were told that, if the AWA policy was to work, they would have to "walk the talk."

The success of the AWA program relies on open and honest communication by all parties. The onus is on the employee to present a business case for the AWA. The manager must ensure that the employee understands the specific client and organizational needs that must also be met. With everything on the table, the manager and employee can design a specific AWA request. The Diversity Advisory Council representative and human resources often serve as a resource and link in the discussion.

This process ensures that E&Y client service will not be negatively affected, that the AWA is consistent with the firm's core values, and what potential issues are addressed up front.

A typical AWA request will include:

- A description of the alternative work arrangement

- The expected hours of work

- Proposed solutions to issues identified

- Proposed communication to other staff and clients

- Measurement/success standards of the AWA

- A pre-agreed notice period for dissolving the arrangement

Some AWAs will ultimately affect the workings of others in the department. This could result in changes to the work flow and group structure. Thus the manager involved in the AWA discussion will need to ensure that the needs of other employees are also met as the AWA is introduced.

Once an AWA has been approved, it is the responsibility of the staff member's manager to monitor the agreement to ensure that client expectations and other commitments such as chargeable hours are being met. This will enable both sides of the agreement to request modifications to the AWA.

Other Best Practices in Accommodation

The following is a list of other best practices in the area of accommodation that can be found in some of the fairest employment systems.

- A Dependent Care Connection service, that allows employees with children access to referrals of reputable child care services, schools, summer camps, special needs, and eldercare placement.

- In-home emergency child care services for staff members who must work overtime hours unexpectedly.

- Emergency backup child care for employees when regular child-care arrangements are unavailable.

- An Overtime Watch Report to ensure employees working 20 percent or more in overtime are taking more than the average amount of time off.

- A corporate fitness discount program for health club membership and their families.

- On-site child-care centres for all employees.

- Family and personal days, i.e., one and one-half days of sick leave a month that can be used either for themselves or for the care of an ill spouse of child.

- The purchase of personal computers for home use that are compatible with the office system to encourage "virtual office" opportunities.

- A night-shift project that allows single parents and others taking courses during the day to work at night.

DIVERSE WORK TEAMS

A second characteristic of the fairest employment systems is their ability to capitalize on the benefits of diverse work teams. This allows the organization to solve problems in the most creative and innovative ways. The most equitable employment systems use the team as the basic unit for problem solving and communication. Each team member recognizes his or her responsibility to support and monitor the overall performance of the entire group. Thus team members not only work well together, but they also try to improve on one another's contribution. This develops a synergy by which the team working together is far more effective than the productivity of the sum of a group of individuals.

Wellington Insurance Company

Out of the fairest systems we have identified, Wellington Insurance Company is an organization that best epitomizes the characteristic of effective work teams. Wellington is a relatively small company with fewer than 200 employees. The organization has recently been acquired by Halifax Insurance, thus some of these comments may be more descriptive of the organization before the take-over.

Wellington encouraged the use of teams by moving away from formal job descriptions. Employees were given job accountabilities that were monitored annually. At the end of each year, each team member would sit down with her or his leader and plan what she or he would accomplish during the next year. The process included quarterly revisions and updates to ensure that the accountabilities were progressing as planned.

Each Wellington employee understood that there was a "floor" to the agreed-upon accomplishments but there was no "ceiling." Employees could participate in activities that fell outside their traditional accountabilities because there was no formal job description to limit their realm of experience. This was significantly different than the autocratic hierarchy found in many traditional organizations, a hierarchy that requires a very strict assignment of job responsibilities and little "cross-pollination" of ideas.

Wellington has moved past the outdated concept of "managers" to the more inclusive title of "team leaders." Employees are a critical part of the decision-making process and are individually responsible and accountable for results. The organization has pursued an aggressive profit-sharing program that encourages every employee to recognize how his or her actions will affect the bottom line. The organization has found that the peer pressure to be productive is far more effective than the old style of management pressure. In one employee's words, "It becomes in vogue to produce."

All Wellington jobs are posted internally to encourage employees to move laterally and acquire the necessary training for other team assignments. The team concept also allows employees to move from one practice area to another. It is not unheard of to talk to employees who started in the mail room and a few years later are commercial underwriters in one of the company's major business units. One employee spoke about moving from claims adjusting to the information services department, a move that would be almost impossible in most hierarchical organizations.

An important part of Wellington's success with work teams is its attention to training and education of employees. Training policies and opportunities are generous by industry standards. Tuition reimbursements, paid study leaves, and bonuses for passing courses are some of the elements of the program. Life-long learning is a core corporate value that allows employees to gain the necessary skills to take on future assignments. Much of the training is also provided internally, allowing employees easier access.

Wellington has created an environment that is dedicated to employee performance. It has linked employee performance to superior customer service, a move that has substantially affected the bottom line. Since moving to this new team-oriented approach, the organization has moved in profit measurement from tenth place against comparator companies to fifth place in less than five years. It has also achieved the goal of zero errors and zero backlogs in processing claims. The organization clearly sets the standard for the business case for equity in the insurance industry.

Other Best Practices in Effective Work Teams

A review of the fairest employment systems will also find the following best practices.

- A formal mentoring program for staff from varied backgrounds.

- Special "bridging programs" designed to introduce employees to non-traditional job opportunities.

- In-house training programs regarding after-tax profits, cash flow, and other accounting basics such as how to read a balance sheet.

- Employee stock ownership plans to encourage employees to share in the financial risks and rewards of the organization.

- Special share offerings and internal trading opportunities for employees.

- Consensus management, where employees decide on the route to take and the team leader takes accountability for the result.

- Quarterly "town-hall" meetings with all employees to discuss the business, including questions to and answers from senior executives.

- A lifestyle committee, which has resulted in subsidized public transportation passes, personal investment seminars, and increasing frequency of employee communications.

- A leave-of-absence policy that can be used to take advantage of situations such as educational sabbaticals, time in a foreign country, and training for athletic competition.

EQUITABLE OPPORTUNITY

A third characteristic of the fairest employment systems is that the organizations seek to hire, promote, and down-size on the basis of merit and skills. In order to do this the organization attempts to remove forms of attitudinal and systemic discrimination that frequently thwart a merit-based system. Such an organization also attempts to remove as many subjective, non-job-related factors from employment decisions in favour of a more objective, systematic approach.

Earlier we identified the types of attitudinal discrimination that could occur in employment systems. Attitudinal discrimination can sometimes be based on stereotypes or prejudices against certain groups. It is difficult for an organization to uncover such bias without the use of a properly designed opinion survey. Nevertheless such attitudes can lead to inequitable treatment of employees.

Systemic discrimination is usually much easier to identify and remove. It will be embedded in long-standing organizational policies and practices. These policies may appear to be fair on the surface but could actually have a negative effect on certain groups. An example of systemic discrimination could be a non-bona fide job requirement—e.g., asking for Canadian experience on a job could discriminate against a qualified candidate with foreign experience.

The fairest employment systems attempt to design formal recruitment and selection systems that ensure the organization attracts the most qualified candidates from all segments of the applicant pool. As we have mentioned many times in this book, equitable organizations seek to do this to remain productive and competitive in the marketplace. A formal recruitment and selection system begins by determining job-related qualifications and then designs a selection process that assesses candidates against these qualifications. This process will also identify the specific behaviours that are reliable predictors of a candidate's ability to perform essential job duties.

The CASCO Selection Process

One example of a best practice in the area of equitable opportunity is the selection process designed by a leading corn miller in Ontario, CASCO. CASCO employs approximately 500 people in the southern Ontario region. Five years ago, the organization set a goal of becoming the employer of choice for the corn products industry. To achieve this goal, the organization has introduced a progressive selection process.

The CASCO selection process was developed to ensure the company was selecting the best qualified individuals to fill all job openings. The process is designed to do this by using position-related facts and data and creating an open and consistent method of supporting employees to achieve career aspirations.

There are five major aspects of the CASCO selection process. They are:

- All job opportunities posted

- Standardized selection instructions

- Candidates considered on the basis of facts and data

- Feedback provided to all candidates

- Specific rules defined

This process allows CASCO management to avoid the most common forms of attitudinal and systemic discrimination usually found in a selection process. The process seeks to identify the transferable skills necessary for a particular job and to match them to the qualifications of candidates. Each job has its own employment requirements and transferable skills. These specific requirements are defined by the department manager, who takes into account

CASCO's current business objectives, production plans, sales volumes, operating efficiencies, and technical innovations when forecasting human resource needs. Thus the CASCO selection process is a dynamic exercise that is responsive to the changing needs of the business. Most selection practices rely on outdated job descriptions that are rarely updated by an organization.

Another outstanding characteristic of the CASCO selection process is its reliance on qualified available human resources. What the company requires is compared to what is available in terms of numbers, skills, and job categories. Thus the organization has collected data about the composition and size of the internal work force. This allows CASCO to achieve the optimum deployment of individuals, based on knowledge, experience, skills, talents, and capabilities.

Equitable opportunity for employees and potential employees is a consistent characteristic of fair employment systems. Achieving this will require a concerted effort at producing an unbiased, objective selection process such as the system being used in CASCO. Such a system does not just happen, it must be created. It also requires education for managers on how to use the system. It will also require communication to staff to ensure that there is a full understanding of how to use the process effectively.

Other Best Practices of Equitable Opportunity

- Totally open job posting for all positions, including in-house advertising centrally located on electronic bulletin boards.

- An employees skills inventory that outlines transferable skills of all staff across the organization.

- Advising external recruitment agencies of the requirement for non-discriminatory recruitment and interest in interviewing qualified candidates from diverse backgrounds.

- Minimizing the influence of word-of-mouth referrals that may reinforce a "who you know" systemic barrier or "nepotism" as an attitudinal barrier.

- Reduced reliance on "walk-in" recruitment.

- Partnerships with non-traditional recruitment organizations that provide employment-related services to various groups.

- Advertising in ethnocultural newspapers and ensuring that text and pictures do not depict employees in stereotypical ways.

- Alliances with professional associations to establish the transferability of foreign credentials.

- A national diversity forum with a group of local, regional recruitment committees to share qualified internal candidates.

- A formal mentoring program for new staff from varied backgrounds who may require support.

- Career counselling and relocation assistance for the spouses of new staff.

DIGNITY AND RESPECT

The final tangible characteristic of the fairest employment systems is the propensity to treat all employees with dignity and respect. This translates into organizations that attempt to create harassment- and discrimination-free environments. In such environments, any complaint of harassment and discrimination is considered a serious matter. Complaints are investigated confidentially and discipline and other corrective action are taken where complaints are substantiated.

Another hallmark of dignity and respect is how people are listened to regardless of rank, age, background, race, sexual orientation, gender, or other perceivable difference. Employee feedback is not only sought but also considered in the ongoing workings of the organization. In some organizations this means "360-degree" feedback, where management performance is actually guided by employee analysis.

IBM — Respect for the Individual

IBM is an organization that effectively demonstrates the characteristics of dignity and respect. One of three core IBM beliefs, since its inception, is "Respect for the Individual." The meaning of this term has evolved since it was first established by IBM visionary Thomas J. Watson Sr. in 1914. Then it meant giving full consideration to the individual employee. By 1963 Thomas J. Watson Jr. in his booklet *A Business and Its Beliefs* carried the term further. He stated, "I believe the real difference between success and failure in a corporation can very often be traced to the question of how well the organization brings out the great energies and talents of its people."

In 1992, IBM conducted a leadership training program across the country entitled "Back to the Future." The major purpose of this seminar was to revisit the basic IBM beliefs and reinforce their relevance in the new business environment. Leaders of the organization were invited to see "respect for the individual" as acknowledging and valuing differences that people bring into the work force–in other words, diversity. IBM instituted a diversity council that was mandated "To create an environment which acknowledges, values, and optimizes the unique capabilities each individual can contribute in working together towards the success of IBM."

In order to create this environment, IBM conducted employee feedback surveys to determine concerns about sexism, racism, harassment, and reverse discrimination. According to Pam Odam, chairperson of the IBM Diversity Council, some critical issues were identified relating to gender. This prompted the council to conduct a more focused study on issues related to women in IBM.

The study looked at both the quantitative and qualitative elements of the issues surrounding gender equity. An analysis was made of the representation of women in leadership roles within the organization. IBM did not use representation numbers as the focus of the diversity program; they were merely external signals of change. The committee sought to identify the reasons for the numbers and then identify solutions to the problems they brought to light.

One of the council's guiding principles was to be inclusive and create win-win scenarios for men and women at IBM. Thus, it was communicated that the advisory council would not be concentrating solely on "women's issues." To support this, one of

the first recommendations of the council was to pursue awareness training on the issues surrounding diversity. In less than
three years, more than 8,000 IBM employees were taken through
a full-day educational program called Valuing Diversity. In some
cases, the organization rented huge banquet halls that allowed
up to 500 IBM employees to participate at the same time.

In order to keep the message and learning current, IBM supported the training with an aggressive communications strategy.
This strategy included videos, a poster campaign, and speeches
by IBM opinion leaders that stressed the principles of IBM diversity. These principles also guided the workings of the Diversity
Council.

These principles are:

• None of us is as strong as all of us.

• Actions will be win-win.

• Diversity encompasses all of our differences.

• The business will benefit.

• We will make a difference.

• Open communication is valued.

• Listening and sharing—internally and externally—is the goal.

IBM has clearly articulated its intention to get to a Five. The
organization realizes that this cannot be done without the participation of its work force. The employees will create an environment in which dignity and mutual respect are valued. Such
an environment does not just happen because it has been mandated by someone in Executive Row.

IBM has also recognized that creating this environment
requires opinion leaders, such as managers and supervisors, to
set the example. Thus the organization has given these leaders
the freedom to accommodate the different needs of individuals
instead of treating everyone and every situation equally. Prior to
the diversity initiative, many IBM managers held the belief that
they had to treat everyone the same. They have now learned that
the organization supports different treatment as long as it

means people are being treated equitably. What is important to an employee who is a single mother may be different to an employee with eldercare responsibilities, but both are legitimate needs to be accommodated.

The message of dignity and mutual respect has been well received within IBM and it continues to live in the organization because it is supported by key communication vehicles, key deliverables, and a relentless commitment to education.

Other Best Practices in Dignity and Mutual Respect

- A confidential hotline for workplace harassment complaints to an external counsellor.

- A harassment mediation service to resolve complaints before the formal process is instituted.

- Special training for managers in non-directive listening and objective investigation techniques to resolve harassment complaints.

- A code of ethics that is integrated and reinforced in every company-sponsored training program.

- A "three-metre rule" by which employees are asked to acknowledge each other by name if they are within three metres of one another.

- A totally open electronic mail system that encourages employees to communicate directly and immediately to the CEO or other senior executives regarding mutual respect concerns.

- An "Open Door Department" where employees can express concerns that, for one reason or another, they're not comfortable bringing to their supervisor.

- External Employment Assistance Programs that stress confidentiality and start with a "first step" hotline to deal with employees' personal problems anonymously.

- Gender-awareness educational program to help employees appreciate the working differences between men and women.

- Training focused on cultural differences in customer service.

- A "Take Our Daughters to Work Day," which exposes the daughters of employees to non-traditional job opportunities for women.

SUMMARY

It is impossible to outline all the characteristics of the "fairest in the land." These are highly complex and dynamic organizations that are continuously changing to meet the needs of the business environment. Suffice to say that these organizations are conscious of the need to create fairer employment systems, not because a government is forcing them to but because they feel it is better for their business.

How fair is your organization? How does it stack up against the fairest in the land? Is equitable opportunity a priority? Do the needs of employees get accommodated? Are diverse work teams operating effectively? Do people have to endure poisoned work environments? These are legitimate questions to ask if you are interested in moving forward on the equity continuum.

On the following pages we present a Diversity Performance Grid. This simple tool can be an effective way for you to establish where your organization may be on the four factors outlined in this chapter. Where does your organization fall? You will remember that we have identified few if any Fives in our research.

Are you a Five?

DIVERSITY PERFORMANCE GRID

Factor 1 – Equitable Opportunity

- Treating people on the basis of merit and skill – hiring, promoting, placing on projects, etc. Specific gender issues to address.

Factor 2 – Accommodation

- Openly attempting to accommodate differing needs of people, including the need to balance work and personal life.

Factor 3 – Work Teams

- Capitalizing on the benefits of diverse work teams to solve problems in the most creative and innovative way.

Factor 4 – Dignity and Respect

- Treating people with dignity and respect. Listening to people regardless of rank, PSA, age, background, colour, sexual orientation, gender, etc.

DIVERSITY PERFORMANCE GRID

Factors for Evaluation	ONE	TWO	THREE	FOUR	FIVE
Factor #1 Equitable Opportunity	Stays within human rights guidelines in hiring and promotion but actively excludes others because of personal bias.	Exhibits protectionism. Hires tokens.	Seeks to hire and promote the best.	Seeks to actively remove inequities in the systems.	Consistently hires and promotes the best, takes a lead role in ensuring others do, and takes a leadership role in improving inequalities in the system.
Factor #2 Accommodation	Denies the existence of work/lifestyle issues.	Acknowledges work/lifestyle issues but discourages use for "business" reasons.	Work/lifestyle arrangements encouraged for business reasons.	Strong advocate for work/lifestyle arrangements. Managers trained in non-traditional options.	Accommodation arrangements integrated into business plan.
Factor #3 Diverse Work Teams	Highly ineffective interactions with diverse team members. Provides no coaching.	Avoids interactions with diverse team members. Ineffective coaching.	Passively includes diverse team members. Some coaching begun.	Actively includes diverse team members. Provides coaching based on individual needs.	Values and capitalizes on teams, diverse skills and backgrounds. Actively provides effective coaching.
Factor #4 Dignity and Respect	Overtly and covertly harasses and discriminates. Defensive.	Covertly harasses and discriminates. Not interested in feedback.	Confronts harassment and discrimination. Listens to feedback.	Proactive measures to prevent harassment and discrimination. Accepts feedback and takes action.	Insists on and demonstrates total dignity and respect. Continually seeks improvement through employee feedback.

INDEX

VIRTUAL DIVERSITY MANAGEMENT FORUM

The Virtual Diversity Management Forum is a complimentary service of TWI Inc. The forum is designed to assist managers in accessing information and support concerning typical diversity issues such as: alternative work arrangements, workplace harassment, religious holidays, litigated equity and alternative dispute resolution.

The forum offers managers support in two separate ways. Managers who register for the forum's **Virtual Clipping Service** will receive (by E-mail) pertinent articles concerning the most pressing diversity issues of the day. The clipping service will allow managers to identify which issues they would like to monitor in order to keep abreast of the fast changing diversity field.

A second feature of the Virtual Diversity Management Forum is the **Diversity Dialogue Groups**. As the North American workforce becomes more diverse, managers must shift from an equal to an equitable leadership style. This shift will cause a new set of management challenges as leaders attempt to accommodate the diverse needs of their workforce. The diversity dialogue groups will allow forum members to dialogue with other managers facing similar challenges in a diverse workforce.

Register for the Virtual Diversity Management Forum

Name & Position: _____

Company: _____

Phone#:_____ Fax#: _____

E-mail:_____

Mailing Address: _____

_____

Please forward to TWI Inc. (416)368-1968, F(416)368-1954, twilson@diversityatwork.com